D0073352

Seamus Heaney

Twayne's English Authors Series

Kinley E. Roby, Editor

Northeastern University

TEAS 468

SEAMUS HEANEY
(1939–   )
Photograph by Albert Fenton

Seamus Heaney

By Thomas C. Foster

University of Michigan–Flint

Twayne Publishers

A Division of G.K. Hall & Co. • Boston

Seamus Heaney
Thomas C. Foster

Published by Twayne Publishers
A Division of G. K. Hall & Co.
70 Lincoln Street
Boston, Massachusetts 02111

Copyediting supervised by Barbara Sutton
Book production by Patricia D'Agostino
Book design by Barbara Anderson

Typeset in 11 pt. Garamond
by Huron Valley Graphics, Inc.

Printed on permanent/durable acid-free paper
and bound in the United States of America

Library of Congress Cataloging-in-Publication Data

Foster, Thomas C.
Seamus Heaney / by Thomas C. Foster.
p. cm.—(Twayne's English authors series ; TEAS 468)
Bibliography: p.
Includes index.
ISBN 0-8057-6984-6 (alk. paper)
1. Heaney, Seamus—Criticism and interpretation. I. Title.
II. Series.
PR6058.E2Z66 1989
821′.914—dc20 89-2149
CIP

For Brenda,
with all my love

Contents

About the Author

Thomas C. Foster received his A.B. from Dartmouth College and his M.A. and Ph.D. from Michigan State University. Currently an assistant professor of English at the University of Michigan–Flint, he has also taught at Michigan State University and Kalamazoo College. He is the author of *Form and Society in Modern Literature,* as well as articles on James Joyce, William Faulkner, Philip Larkin, and twentieth-century poetry.

Preface

While evaluating poetry ought not be reduced to the level of handicapping racehorses, Seamus Heaney ranks at the forefront of contemporary poetry. The consistent power and elegance of his verse over two decades has brought him that rare combination of popularity and critical acclaim. First coming to readers' attention in the mid-1960s as part of a remarkable generation of young Northern Irish poets that included Michael Longley, Derek Mahon, Tom Paulin, and James Simmons, Heaney emerged as the preeminent poet of the group a decade later with the publication of his astonishing fourth volume, *North.*

A poet of place, he has grounded his verse in the six counties of Northern Ireland, exploring his agricultural beginnings as well as the violence of the Troubles, the history of conquest by a dizzying array of foreign powers as well as the quiet endurance of the inhabitants—in other words, the entire range of life, love, history, and politics that, as he says, "gives Irish poetry its sex appeal." What has set his work off from the great mass of poetry, not just of Ireland but of any nation, is his tremendous control of the language. Like James Joyce, he hears in words not simply meaning but events, histories, lives. He has delved into the Anglo-Saxon past of English in both diction and poetics to awaken in us an awareness of the cultural consciousness embodied in words. In so doing, he also charges the poetic line with power and tension, playing off a fairly traditional sense of form with a radical sense of prosodic possibilities.

This book seeks to trace the various threads of his poetry as they weave back and forth through his books, for although the subjects and the treatments change from volume to volume, Heaney's themes, concerns, images, and practices crop up time and again. In pursuing this goal, I have had the assistance of the gentleman himself, who very graciously permitted himself to be interviewed on the evening of 14 May 1987 in Cambridge, Massachusetts. Statements by Mr. Heaney that appear in the text without citation are taken from that interview. I only hope that my book proves worthy of its subject.

I also received help in writing this volume from conversations over the years with R. K. Meiners and William A. Johnsen of Michigan

State University and with Evan Watkins of the University of Washington. I feel I must acknowledge the work of the previous critics of Heaney's poetry, particularly Neil Corcoran, whose book is a model of clarity and insight. Finally, there are two people without whom this study would never have come about. To Leonora Smith, of Michigan State University, many thanks for years of discussion, advice, encouragement, and editorial guidance. And to my wife, Brenda, my undying gratitude for the love, support, and understanding that made this book possible.

I would like to acknowledge Faber & Faber Lmt. and Farrar, Straus & Giroux for permission to quote from the works of Seamus Heaney, and to Oxford University Press for permission to quote from *North.*

Thomas C. Foster

University of Michigan–Flint

Chronology

1939	Seamus Justin Heaney born 13 April in County Derry, Northern Ireland.
1939–1953	Heaney family lives at Mossbawn, fifty-acre farm.
1945–1951	Attends local Anahorish school.
1951–1957	Boarder at St. Columb's College, Derry.
1953	Family moves to The Wood, a farm at far end of parish. Seamus's brother Christopher dies and is later subject of "Mid-Term Break."
1957–1961	Attends Queen's College, Belfast, majoring in English language and literature; graduates with first-class honors degree.
1961–1962	Takes postgraduate teacher's training diploma, St. Joseph's College of Education, Andersontown, Belfast.
1963	Lecturer in English at St. Joseph's.
1963–1966	Joins Philip Hobsbaum's "Group," a poetry workshop including Michael Longley, Derek Mahon, Stewart Parker, and James Simmons.
1965	Belfast Festival brings him exposure in *Observer;* publishes *Eleven Poems,* pamphlet, in connection with festival; marries Marie Devlin in August.
1966	*Death of a Naturalist* published and wins Geoffrey Faber Prize, Gregory Award for young writers, and Somerset Maugham Award. Son Michael born in July.
1966–1970	Lecturer in English (modern literature), Queen's University, Belfast.
1968	Son Christopher born in February.
1969	*Door into the Dark.* Discovers P. V. Glob's *The Bog People.*
1970–1971	Guest lecturer, University of California, Berkeley; meets Tom Flanagan (*The Year of the French*) and Conor Cruise O'Brien.
1971	Returns to Northern Ireland in September; writes of ten-

	sion in Ulster at Christmas in the *Listener.*
1972	Bloody Sunday riots in which thirteen civilians are killed by British Army in Derry 30 January. Resigns post at Queen's and moves to cottage at Glanmore, in County Wicklow, to work as full-time freelance writer. *Wintering Out.* Begins translating Old Irish *Buile Sweeney;* meets Robert Lowell.
1973	Fulfills promise made in "The Tollund Man" and visits Aarhus, Denmark, to see the Bog People. Daughter, Catherine Ann, born in April.
1973–1975	Reads heavily in Yeats, Osip Mandelstam, and Dante.
1973–1977	Hosts *Imprint* on Radio Eireann, biweekly, later weekly.
1975	*North* published and wins Duff Cooper Memorial Prize. Lowell visits Glanmore. Begins teaching at Carysfort, a teachers's training college, Dublin.
1976	Moves to house in Sandymount, Dublin; named Department Head in English at Carysfort.
1979	*Field Work.*
1980	*Selected Poems.*
1981	Resigns post at Carysfort; accepts post as visiting professor at Harvard.
1982	With Ted Hughes edits *The Rattle Bag,* poetry anthology for older children; receives honorary D. Litt., Queen's University.
1983	Publishes *Sweeney Astray,* translation of *Buile Suibhne;* cofounds Field Day Publishing with Brian Friel, Tom Paulin, and other; *An Open Letter,* Field Day pamphlet.
1984	Mother, Margaret Kathleen, dies. Open University awards him honorary degree. Elected Boylston Professor of Rhetoric and Oratory, Harvard. *Station Island.*
1984–1987	Divides time between Harvard, teaching one semester per year, and Sandymount.
1987	*The Haw Lantern* published in May.

Chapter One

A Poet in Ulster

Contemporary poetry has probably seen a greater use of the personal details of writers' lives than any other period in history. The whole confessional school—Sylvia Plath, John Berryman, Anne Sexton, Robert Lowell, and the legions of lesser talents who paddle along in their wake—inaugurated an era of intense, often agonizing self-scrutiny in American poetry especially. Yet even on the other side of the Atlantic, poets far removed in sensibility as well as geography from the confessional troupe make great use of their personal histories. One thinks of Philip Larkin's "Whitsun Weddings" or Jon Silkin's great poem "Death of a Son" or even Tony Harrison's often hilarious, often poignant poems of growing up in working-class England. What these poems share, for the most part, is a sense of expiation or assuagement: a cleansing of some dark emotion or memory. Yet there is another possible model for the use of personal experience in poetry, one that is essentially celebratory rather than cathartic. One poet writing such verse is Northern Ireland's Seamus Heaney, whose work records the full range of life—and death—in his native land.

Heaney was born 13 April 1939, on the family farm, called Mossbawn, near Castledawson, County Derry, the eldest of nine children of Patrick and Margaret Kathleen (née McCann) Heaney. He received his early education at the local Anahorish school, from 1945 to 1951, and as a boarder at St. Columb's College in Derry from 1951 to 1957. He has written extensively, both in poetry and essays, about these early years, particularly about the importance of place and the names of places. Life at Mossbawn figures prominently in Heaney's early work, especially, providing the subject matter for the great bulk of his first two volumes: "Churning Day," about the rhythms of a ritual chore; "Death of a Naturalist," about an encounter in a frog pond; "The Early Purges," about culling newborn kittens; "The Outlaw," about an illegally kept bull.

What most of these poems of childhood have in common is the sense of safety, of certainty of place, of belonging to a community. Neighbors understand one another on a personal and agricultural level even if they differ strongly in political and religious beliefs. They maintain a prudent silence regarding points of divergence, limiting their talk (and these are not, especially the men, talkative people) to safe subjects, weather and crops. While those early days may at times be fraught with terror, it is of a manageable sort: angry frogs, dark corners of the barn, the mysteries of life and death in a context where such matters are a daily concern.

Another major factor in his early comfort and safety was the presence of his aunt, Mary Heaney, as part of the family. Heaney has stated that his aunt was a kind of second mother to him, providing him with additional attention and shelter that his mother alone, with nine children in all, would have been unable to offer.[1] She has figured in a number of poems. She is one of the unnamed women in "Churning Day," as well as the dedicatee of the prefatory poems, "Mossbawn," in *North*. She appears later in "In Memoriam: Francis Ledwidge" both as a young girl at the time of Ledwidge's enlistment and death, in which role she serves as an agrarian counterpoint to the violence at the front, and as a woman taking the young Seamus on an excursion to Portstewart, where they see a World War I memorial. Most recently, her handiwork appears: the chestnut tree she planted the year her nephew Seamus was born is the subject of the final sonnet of "Clearances." What Mary Heaney represents in the poetry is sense of community, of stability, even of local memory offered by the traditional rural culture of Northern Ireland. In "The Seed Cutters," for instance, he addresses Breughel, declaring "You'll know them if I can get them true."[2] And indeed, the scene he invokes of a "frieze," of people kneeling as they cut seed potatoes in one of their "calendar customs" could, with changes in clothing, be a painting by the Flemish master. The childhood of the poems, then, stands as a kind of golden age, a childhood

> that was set in what you might call mythic surroundings: well water and harps and scythes and sickles, so that the dedicatory poem in *North* specifically mentions Breughel and specifically mentions "calendar customs" and the Book of Hours and so on and specifically relates that to medieval art forms and codified and ratified modes of cultural seeing. Once you become the kind of person who can see your own childhood as a reenactment of a work of art, you've clearly become self-conscious.

This past innocence appears in the poetry, but often with a cutting edge: the fright of "Death of a Naturalist," the violence of "The Early

Purges." Heaney is also sufficiently self-conscious to avoid overly sentimental representations of those early days.

In 1953 the family moved to the other end of the parish from Mossbawn, to a farm known as The Wood. It was also in 1953 that Heaney's younger brother Christopher was killed in an accident, an event commemorated in the early poem "Mid-Term Break." That poem presents a young Heaney on the verge of manhood at fourteen, confused by the older men's consoling handshakes (as the eldest child, he receives adult treatment), still young enough to have his mother silently hold his hand and to not view the corpse until the next morning. This family tragedy, then, becomes the focal point for a poetic rite of passage, and it stands as one of the very few specific events to appear in his early poetry.

Heaney enrolled at Queen's University, Belfast, in 1957, graduating four years later with a first in English language and literature. Although the department chairman, Peter Butter, urged him to go to Oxford for graduate study, Heaney opted instead for a teacher's training diploma from St. Joseph's College of Education in Belfast, which he took in 1962.[3] The next two years were enormously important in his development as a poet. Following graduation from St. Joseph's, he took a position at St. Thomas's Intermediate School, where the headmaster, short story writer Michael McLaverty, made him aware of the poetry of Patrick Kavanagh. Already drawn to Hopkins and Keats, and having recently discovered several contemporary Irish poets—John Hewitt, Thomas Kinsella, John Montague—as well as the Englishman Ted Hughes, Heaney found in Kavanagh the rural, northern life that suggested to him that his own experience could provide subject matter for poetry. That same year he began to write, and in November the *Belfast Telegraph* published the first poem, "Tractors," which Heaney has never bothered to collect. More significantly, early the following year, "Mid-Term Break," was accepted by the *Kilkenny Magazine,* providing what he describes to Neil Corcoran as "a terrific sense of confirmation."[4] With the beginning of a new school year in 1963, Heaney took a post as lecturer in English at St. Joseph's. That move ultimately brought him into contact with Philip Hobsbaum and the "Group."

Under Hobsbaum's direction—indeed, at his flat—a remarkable group of young poets, which aside from Heaney included James Simmons, Michael Longley, Stewart Parker, and Derek Mahon, began meeting to share their writing in sessions modeled on those of the London "Group" of the fifties and early sixties, which Hobsbaum had also organized and guided. That so many of today's prominent Irish poets should have been in Belfast at that time is certainly remarkable. That Hobsbaum was there is truly fortunate, for he provided the spark and impetus, as Heaney describes in his 1978 *Honest Ulsterman* essay, reprinted in *Preoccupations:*

> He emanated energy, generosity, belief in the community, trust in the parochial, the inept, the unprinted. He was impatient, dogmatic, relentlessly literary: yet he was patient with those he trusted, unpredictably susceptible to a wide variety of poems and personalities and urgent that the social and political exacerbations of our place should disrupt the decorums of literature. If he drove some people mad with his absolutes and hurt others with his overbearing, he confirmed as many with his enthusiasms.[5]

After Hobsbaum departed in 1966, Heaney took over hosting duties until 1970, and during that time the "Group" came to include such younger poets as Frank Ormsby, Michael Foley, and Paul Muldoon.[6] One of the chief achievements of the group was their inclusion in the Belfast Festival of 1965. They received their first outside exposure through Mary Holland's writing in the London *Observer* and through pamphlets of poems by Mahon, Longley, and Heaney.

The following year, in May, the prestigious publishing house of Faber and Faber brought out Heaney's first book, *Death of a Naturalist.* He had sent them, at their request, an earlier book manuscript in January of 1965, which they declined but showed interest in. From there on, as he told Corcoran, things moved very quickly: "So in about four months I wrote a hell of a lot, and I think I sent them another thing in about May or June. I got married in August and we went to London for our honeymoon, and by then they said they were going to take it."[7] And for the next year things happened very swiftly indeed. In August 1965 he married Marie Devlin, from County Tyrone and then a teacher in intermediate school. In May 1966 the book came out, winning the Geoffrey Faber Prize, the Somerset Maugham Award, and the Gregory Award for young writers. In July his son Michael was born, the first of three children. And that autumn he succeeded Hobsbaum as lecturer in English at Queen's University, a post he held until 1970. During that same period he began publishing essays and reviews, first in educational journals and later in more general circulation periodicals such as the *New Statesman,* the *Listener,* and the *Guardian;* these writings, along with his frequent appearances on BBC-radio, Radio

Eireann, and on television have served to make him perhaps the best known contemporary Irish poet among the general public. He has commented on all manner of cultural, artistic, and political affairs, and even appeared on the segment dealing with the Irish dialect of America's PBS series, *The Story of English.*

He also traveled during his time at Queen's, and found himself not in Ulster but in Spain in the summer of 1969 when the current Troubles erupted at home. He has made much both of his time in Spain and of his absence at a critical moment in the poems "Summer 1969," "Summer Home," and "High Summer" and also perhaps in "Exposure," the closing poem in *North.* The crying baby of "High Summer" is his second son, Christopher, born in February 1968. His travels included a guest lectureship in 1970–71 at the University of California at Berkeley, where he met Thomas Flanagan, who later wrote *The Year of the French,* and Conor Cruise O'Brien. Flanagan, who was then the author of a study of nineteenth-century Irish fiction, is the co-dedicatee, with Seamus Deane, of *Preoccupations.*

Two publications in 1969 were especially important in Heaney's career. The first was Faber's issuing of his second book, *Door into the Dark,* in June. The book was tentatively received by reviewers, who sensed in it, rightly, something unsettled and transitional. The second major publication provided Heaney with the material he would need to find his perspective on the violence in Ulster. It was, curiously enough, a study of archaeological finds in Jutland, Denmark, P. V. Glob's astonishing work, *The Bog People.* The book details, with photographs, the discovery of a series of bodies, some of them more than two thousand years old, the victims of tribal justice and ritual sacrifice, their bodies tanned and toughened by the amazing preservative properties of the bogs that Heaney had already noted in "Bogland," the final poem in *Door into the Dark.* What that poem seemed to be searching for was a thematic center, and the combination of the renewed Troubles and Glob's work offered such a center, which Heaney employed in his next two books in a remarkable series of Bog Poems.

Yet finding a point of observation and perspective was something less than a panacea, and his subsequent work has been met with the charge, often from his fellow Northern Catholics, that he has ducked the issue of the violence and repression. He feels the need, as anyone in the situation would, to address, if not the situation itself, at least his own response to that situation, but he is also aware of the dangers involved in writing anything that, in the cause of truth telling, is actually an exacerbation. That is to say, in 1966 I wrote a poem called "Requiem for the Croppies," which is a deliberately espoused nationalist Irish poem about the insurrection of 1798, which was the founding of Irish Republicanism. Now, writing in 1966 in Northern Ireland, where the Unionist hegemony was in position, where there was also a new slight air of liberalism, it was all right for me, and I'm very glad I did it, as a Nationalist minority poet to use the poem to stake an imaginative claim for this sensibility. So the poem did have cultural affiliations, did have political meaning, but it did not have violent implications for the society. It was just saying remember us, take us into account. Twenty years later, that poem, which is about the act of rebellion and the Croppies being killed and sacrifice and violence, can be read as a code poem in support of the IRA, can and has been. Now that's that, it's okay. That poem and the IRA and myself grew out of the same bed, the same heritage. But for me to write that poem now, it would be very different. It would be in fact a poem of violence rather than a poem of imagination. So the second demand that arises is that you beware of the fallout of your words, and perhaps I've been unduly aware of that, of the relationship between lyric and life, of the responsibility for what you say. Geoffrey Hill has three lines in *The Mystery of the Charity of Charles Peguy,* "Must men stand by what they write / as by their camp-beds or their weaponry / or shell-shocked comrades while they sag and cry?" In other words, do you have to take responsibility for the effect of your work? And in the North of Ireland, I think the answer is yes.

He mentions that this is a second demand. The first is, very simply, "to deal somehow with truth and justice," a situation requiring more work of the poet who lives in a society like that of Northern Ireland, where truth and justice "are not generally at work in the society." Looking at Heaney's career, one notices that the most inflammatory poems, "Docker" say, are those written before the outbreak of the Troubles, and that the eruption of violence seems to have made him more cautious in his choice of words. Not his choice of subjects. He has written about a good many aspects of the hostilities—terrorists and victims, journalists and the phraseology with which they make horror palatable to the evening news audience, activists and bystanders. His handling of that material, however, while clearly informed by his religious and political and personal background, has been conscientiously even-handed.

In September 1971 Heaney returned with his family to Belfast, where conditions were rapidly worsening. In a piece of the *Listener* entitled "Christmas 1971" he recounts the increasing military presence, including his own experience of being pulled over by the Army for having let his car tax lapse. "It hasn't been named martial law," he writes, "but that's what it feels like." In that essay, reprinted in *Preoccupations,* he notes the twin threats of Protestant vigilantes and IRA Provisionals, each with their slogans, bombs, and gunmen. There is in that short essay a sense of something about to happen, of all forces lined up and waiting.

Less than a month later, the other shoe dropped. On 30 January 1972 thirteen civilians were killed in Derry in clashes with the British Army: the tragedy was known as Bloody Sunday. What had previously been martial law in effect now became something much more like guerrilla warfare. On a wall in Belfast, printed like a football score, was the tally: "PARAS THIRTEEN, BOGSIDE NIL." In reprisal, the Provos stepped up their bombing attacks. (The IRA Provisionals—Provos—and the paramilitary Royal Ulster Constabulary have conspired in a reign of terror in Northern Ireland. The Provos have been particularly successful in enforcing their will within the Catholic community by use of the bomb-enforced curfew.) One such act led to Heaney's most beautifully moving elegy, "Casualty," when his acquaintance Louis O'Neill was killed when a bomb exploded in a Protestant bar. Indeed, both that volume, *Field Work,* and *Station Island* are filled with victims—and perpetrators—of the ongoing violence: O'Neill; a friend from university and Belfast social worker, Sean Armstrong; Heaney's cousin Colum McCartney; the British ambassador to Ireland, Christopher Ewart-Biggs; a shopkeeper murdered by uniformed members of the security forces; one of the Maze prison hunger-strikers. Being a part of Northern Ireland through the seventies entailed, almost necessarily, an acquaintance with the victims of internecine warfare.

Shortly thereafter, though, Heaney found sanctuary from the immediate bloodshed, if not its aftereffects, when he was offered the cottage at Glanmore in County Wicklow by Ann Saddlemeyer, a Canadian scholar. In August 1972, he resigned his post at Queen's and moved south to work full-time as a freelance writer. At Glanmore he did much of his finest work, which included the poems of *North,* much of *Field Work,* and the first draft translation of the *Buile Suibhne,* which in 1983 he completed as *Sweeney Astray.* His sojourn to Wicklow allowed him the chance to renew his ties to rural life that are so evident in the later poems of that period, especially the "Glanmore Sonnets" themselves, which are dedicated to Saddlemeyer. The four years spent there were eventful in a quiet way. *Wintering Out* appeared shortly after the family moved there, in November 1972. The following year in April his daughter, Catherine Ann, was born. Also in 1973 he made the pilgrimage to Aarhus, Denmark, to view the bog people, as he had promised in "The Tollund Man." During the next two years, he read extensively in Yeats, Dante, and Osip Mandelstam, and those readings helped shape his later writings. In 1975 *North* appeared. It was immediately acclaimed in Britain and America, although less well-received in Ireland and particularly in the North, where the emphasis on violence and tribal mentality did not play well. Nevertheless, the book won the Duff Cooper Memorial Prize in 1976 and stands as his most powerful and most fully realized volume. Another influence came into his life in 1975 when Robert Lowell came to visit after a conference in Kilkenny. Although Lowell's impact on the poetry is for the most part indirect and short-lived, Heaney's admiration of him shows through in *Field Work,* which also contains an elegy for him.

In the autumn of 1975, feeling the need for a steadier source of income and wishing to purchase a house in Dublin, Heaney began teaching full-time at Carysfort College of Education. In November of the following year he moved the family to a house in Sandymount, Dublin, where they still reside. He chaired the English Department at Carysfort from 1976 until 1981. In 1979 he published *Field Work,* which further cemented his reputation in the United States. He also spent a term teaching at Harvard, which was to become the first of many.

In 1981 Heaney resigned his position at Carysfort, and in January of the following year he accepted a five-year contract at Harvard to teach half of each year. In 1984 he was named Boylston Professor of Oratory and Rhetoric, a post traditionally held by poets. His poetry workshop, as he explained to Neil Corcoran, is very much on the model of the Belfast Group, except that rather than being one among equals, he is now the center of action as well as the authority figure.[8] Since the position only ties him down for four months of the year, its great advantage over his post at Carysfort is that it frees him for the other eight months. The move also fit into a sort of habitual rootlessness: "I'm old enough now to see a pattern in myself of displacing myself from situations that were established. I've moved, moved, moved, moved. It's basically a distrust of comfort. I believe in comfort but I distrust it."

His years at Harvard have proved to be quite productive. In 1982 he and Ted Hughes co-edited *The Rattle Bag,* a wonderful poetry anthology for children. In 1983 he started, with playwright Brian Friel, poets Tom Paulin and Seamus Deane, and others, Field Day Publishing, an outgrowth of Field Day Theatre, founded by Friel and actor Stephen Rea. The theater's first production in 1980 in Derry was Friel's *Translations,* which follows the language conflict between Irish and English during the English survey of Ireland in 1833. Its themes and attitudes are familiar to the readers of Heaney's verse, and they set the tone for much of the work at Field Day: historical awareness, sensitivity to the interrelationship between England and Ireland, yet a firm sense of a single Irish identity:

> When we started Field Day, I liked the idea of it [*Sweeney Astray*] being published in Derry. It's a kind of all-Ireland event situated just within the North, and there's a little bit of political naughtiness in that. This was one of the reasons I translated the placenames into their modern equivalents. I hoped that gradually the Northern Unionist or Northern Protestant readership might, in some minuscule way, feel free to identify with the Gaelic tradition.[9]

Sweeney Astray appeared from Field Day in 1983, although its publication in England and America was delayed until 1984 to coincide with that of *Station Island.*

His other Field Day publication has been *An Open Letter,* a pamphlet poem in which he mischievously objects to his inclusion as a "British" writer in the 1982 *Penguin Book of Contemporary British Poetry.* While the pamphlet stirred a good deal of attention, Heaney shrugs off its publication, telling Corcoran he partially regrets having written it, later laughing it off as a flight of whimsy.[10] The vacillation is characteristic, as is the underlying sentiment not to be regarded too lightly as a product of empire.

Heaney delivered the Peter Laver Memorial Lecture at Grasmere in August 1984. In that address, "Place and Displacement: Recent Poetry of Northern Ireland," he discusses the dynamics of writing poetry in Ulster through attention to the work of Derek Mahon, Paul Muldoon, and Michael Longley. His models here are Wordsworth's response to his psychological crisis when England, to which he was loyal, declared war upon Revolutionary France, of which he was greatly enamored, and the Jungian notion of surmounting "insoluble conflict" by, as Anthony Storr has it, "developing a 'new level of consciousness' " with which to confront that dilemma.[11] He notes that both Catholic and Protestant in that troubled province live in a kind of exile, a land neither England nor Ireland, observing that "the condition is chronic and quotidian and not necessarily terminal" (*P&D,* 5). In such a context, he insists on two points, first, "the profound relationship between poetic technique and the historical situation. It is a superficial response to the work of Northern Irish poets to conceive of their lyric stances as evasions of the actual conditions." He goes on to suggest that technique is an internalized and more complex response to social crisis than, say, "the protest poetry of the sixties." The second point is that even if the poem operates in a plane other than the political, that aesthetic level

> does not absolve it or the poet from political status. . . . Pure poetry is perfectly justifiable in earshot of the carbomb but it still implies a politics, depending on the nature of the poetry. A poetry of hermetic wit, of riddles and slips and self-mocking ironies, while it may appear culpably miniaturist or fastidious to the activist with his microphone at the street corner, may be exercising in its inaudible way a fierce disdain of the amplified message, or a distressed sympathy with it. (*P&D,* 7–8)

There is something of self-justification here, of answering critics who find him evasive or uncertain in the matter of politics or who criticize the well-made poem approach to craft in the face of social upheaval. Still, one need not be surprised that poets who honed their craft together, as these men did in the Group, would opt for similar, if distinct, approaches to the insoluble problem of strife and violence in their homeland. Nor should we find it odd that commentators like Christopher Ricks have noted similar language strategies between these contemporary poets and the English metaphysical poet Andrew Marvell, composing during another period of civil war. The lyric, Heaney argues, will find its own route, its own logic, by which it will discover its own solutions.

One of the chief features of *The Haw Lantern,* which appeared in 1987, is Heaney's renewed tie to his childhood, particularly in the sonnet sequence "Clearances," written in memory of his mother, who died in 1984. The poem returns to the farm life of his childhood that he has explored so often, particularly in the early books, although here from a clearly more mature and ruminative perspective. The book is also characterized by a new type of poem, whose genesis he credits in part to his time in America:

> I would say that the distance and the slight permissiveness, the slightly gravityless life that I've had here has in some way freed me to be more chancy in writing. In the new book there are some poems that are parable poems;

there's a poem called "From the Frontier of Writing" which uses an encounter at a roadblock, a kind of archetypal Ulster, Catholic situation. It turns it into a parable inquisition and escape and freedom implicit in a certain kind of lyric poem. You know, as you cross the bar and you're free into that other region. So I would say the American experience may have confirmed and assisted what I think happens anyway as you get toward your fifties; that is, a certain rethinking of yourself, a certain distance from your first self.

The physical distance from both family and origin of his residency at Harvard, then, reinforces for him the psychic and temporal distance he has traveled. That he should undertake allegory certainly indicates a change of direction and a large element of risk-taking; clearly, his arrival at the end of *Station Island* at "the font of exhaustion" proved to be only a temporary matter. Corcoran very accurately observes that both in its title sequence and in the self-allusiveness of the "Sweeney Redivivus" poems the previous book contained a large dose of stock-taking and summing-up. Yet middle age is Januslike, facing both backward toward a more youthful self and forward toward something new, if as yet undetermined. Nostalgia, the refusal to take the risks embodied in the future, Heaney politely declines. *The Haw Lantern* looks resolutely forward, promising new growth in an already major poet.

Chapter Two

Learning the Craft: *Death of a Naturalist* and *Door into the Dark*

Death of a Naturalist

In his essay on William Butler Yeats in *Fables of Identity,* Northrop Frye makes a distinction between a "growing" poet like Yeats, who constantly struggles to achieve his mature poetic, and an "unfolding" poet such as Dante, who simply opens into his voice and form. Arguing that the difference lies in the breakdown of mythic and poetic language between Dante's time and Yeats's, Frye presents these different versions of poetic life as mutually exclusive. Certainly they present a dichotomy, yet perhaps elements of both may exist simultaneously in a single poet's career. In the case of Seamus Heaney, for instance, his first books suggest that while many aspects must wait for growth and development, numerous crucial elements of his mature verse are intact from his earliest poems.

The most striking feature of Heaney's early work, particularly for the reader coming to it from *North* or *Station Island,* is the strength of the language. Compare, for example, these two evocations of morning:

> Clouds ran their wet mortar, plastered the daybreak
> Grey. The stones clicked tartly
> If we missed the sleepers but mostly
> Silent we headed up the railway . . . [1]

and

> Morning stir in the hostel. A pot
> hooked on forged links. Soot flakes. Plumping water.
> The open door letting in sunlight.
> Hearthsmoke rambling and a thud of earthenware . . . [2]

The first, the opening of "Dawn Shoot," is from his first book, *Death of a Naturalist* (1966), the second is from *Station Island,* published eighteen years later. In each opening the poet presents a highly sensuous rendering of his surroundings, made more concrete by the solidity of his sometimes surprising word choice. Clouds "plaster" the daybreak and the stones' click is "tart" in the first, while smoke "rambles" and water "plumps" in the second. There is great emphasis here on onomatopoeia, both in these phrases and in the hushed sibilance of the third and fourth lines of "Dawn Shoot." Heaney has never shied from conventional poetic devices.

At the same time, however, this poem, like so many in this volume and later, plays off a tension between that "poetic" language and the conversational, ordinary language of the speaker and his friend:

> There was the playboy trotting up to the hole
> By the ash tree, "Wild rover no more,"
> Said Donnelly and emptied two barrels
> And got him. I finished him off.
>
> (*DN,* 30)

Here there is a self-conscious division between the two modes; the poet employs "literary" devices in his descriptions of the morning and especially of the birds—the corncrake, snipe, and cock—while narrating the actual shooting and the exchanges between the speaker and Donnelly in a flatter, prosaic verse. Often, in this first volume and the one that follows, that split between the two modes of writing seems awkward, forced, or arbitrary. The commonplace language may be too chummy, as in the line "By God, the old man could handle a spade" (*DN,* 13) from "Digging," while the crafted language may call too much attention to its craft, as in the overwrought opening lines of "Mid-Term Break": "I sat all morning in the college sick bay / Counting bells knelling classes to a close" (*DN,* 28). One of the great developments of his mature work is the increasing ability to integrate the tightly packed literary language with the looser forms of speech in order to exploit the tension between the two more fully.

Not only is the kind of language already established in this first volume, but so are many of Heaney's pet words and images. In the marvelous "Churning Day" we are treated to "plumping kettles," crocks like "large pottery bombs," the "plash and gurgle" of the milk, and the "pat and slap" of the butter spades. These words, sounds, images will recur throughout his later work. Of particular interest is the intrusion of violence, in the pottery bombs, into this domestic and tranquil realm, three years prior to the start of the current Troubles in 1969. Nor is it an isolated occurrence. *Death of a Naturalist* testifies throughout to the small-scale violence of rural life; this is no poetry for agrarian sentimentalists. Its implicit, sometimes explicit, perils may threaten the poet's younger self, as in the title poem or "The Early Purges," yet he presents that world without flinch or apology. "Churning Day" also presents a characteristic rhythm to which Heaney will return again and again:

> My mother took first turn, set up rhythms
> that slugged and thumped for hours. Arms ached.
> Hands blistered. Cheeks and clothes were spattered
> with flabby milk.
>
> (*DN*, 21)

The first sentence, comparatively open with its run-on line end, gives way to not one but two terse, two word sentences, each consisting of a noun and a strong verb. Later modifications, as in the opening of poem 10 from the "Station Island" sequence, may substitute a modifier for either element, but especially the verb. In any event, the pair of short sentences used as punctuation is already a standard feature in Heaney's first book of poetry.

At the same time "Churning Day" also points to one of the weaknesses of Heaney's early verse. Nearly all the poems in these first two volumes grow out of his domestic, familiar, juvenile world and deal with life on and around a County Derry farm. Heaney has said that his career as a poet began "when my roots were crossed with my reading" (*P*, 37). That reading, especially Gerard Manley Hopkins, William Wordsworth, Patrick Kavanagh, and Ted Hughes, valorized the use of local, personal, rural, natural subjects for poetry and sanctioned the young poet's use of his own background as material for his verse.

This heavily romantic reading pushes him to find transcendent meaning in life on the farm, with the result that many poems are crushed under a symbolic or psychological freight they simply cannot bear. "The Barn" seems a notably weak instance of this tendency:

> The dark gulfed like a roof-space. I was chaff
> To be pecked up when birds shot through the air-slits.

I lay face-down to shun the fear above.
The two-lugged sacks moved in like great blind rats.
(*DN,* 17)

What is the purpose of the misapplication of the verb "gulfed," normally a transitive verb, here used intransitively? It appears that Heaney has used it only to call attention to itself. Moreover, that first sentence contains a howling tautology: the dark is not *like* a roof-space, it *is* a roof-space, the setting being the interior of the barn. Similarly, the assertion "I was chaff / To be pecked up" is a sudden and arbitrary image, not prepared for earlier in the poem. Why is he chaff? What is the justification for this feeling? We never know. The pose, however attractive, is simply a pose, a poetlike act. As if to underscore the artificiality, Heaney's versification deserts him in this final stanza. Because of the three major breaks, two of them at line ends, the stanza falters along with little sense of purpose. Moreover, the scansion, especially of the second line, adds to the stumbling quality. How are we to read a line with two anapests ("To be pecked," "up when birds") followed immediately by two spondees ("shot through," "air-slits"), which are themselves separated only by the unaccented syllable "the"? There are simply two many stresses in awkward spots, given the utter regularity of the following line. Simply put, many of these early poems strive too hard to add a significance rather than to allow the scene to find its own importance.

Some poems, certainly, are capable enough. "At a Potato Digging" can support the racial memory of horror precisely because the activity of digging potatoes recalls the horror invoked. From its opening line, "A mechanical digger wrecks the drill," both the meaning and the diction point to a violence inherent in the apparently peaceful life of the countryside, where farmers struggle to pluck their livelihood from the soil. Here the mangled syntax he learns from Hopkins and Anglo-Saxon poetry—the alliteration of hard consonants, the stacking of stresses in a line such as "Li*k*e *c*rows atta*ck*ing *c*row-bla*ck* fields, they stretch"—finds appropriate place. Indeed, the problems in this poem arise when he opens up the diction, as in the second movement (the poem is in four movements), he offers up the feeble line "Good smells exude from crumbled earth." Yet later this same ground remains "faithless," unreliable, despite the intervening century or so between the famine and the composition of the poem. Even when the workers take their lunch break, their motions suggest the deaths brought on by the famine: the "rhythm deadens" as they end their morning's work, which has left them "Dead-beat" as they "flop / Down in the ditch," an action that suggests both the clay pits where the harvest rotted and the mass graves of the "Millions who rotted with it." Small wonder, then, that the work takes on religious implications:

> Heads bow, trunks bend, hands fumble towards the black
> Mother. Processional stooping through the turf
>
> Recurs mindlessly as autumn. Centuries
> Of fear and homage to the famine god
> Toughen the muscles behind their humbled knees,
> Make a seasonal altar of the sod.
>
> (*DN,* 31)

The passage bears the stamp of mastery that is no less impressive for being only occasionally realized in this volume. Heaney employs the line break brilliantly in delaying the key word "Mother." This poem stands as his earliest invocation of the earth as mother-goddess-lover, demanding tribute, worship, sacrifice, as it is of kneeling or stooping as a characteristic Irish position. Still, the act of obeisance, though it may recur mindlessly, acts not to break the spirit or the body but to "Toughen the muscles behind their humbled knees." Heaney recognizes the dignity in the humility, and throughout his career he maintains a fascination with and respect for those who, unlike himself, practice the timeless rituals of work and faith.

Indeed, from the first poem in the book, Heaney articulates a respect for and kinship with those who dig in the earth. That poem, "Digging," while full of missteps, lays out a course for the poet's work from which he has rarely wavered. In the first stanza the "squat pen" sits "snug as a gun" (*DN,* 13). The implied violence of the activity of writing fails, comes across as forced, overblown. But then the poem launches straight into a discussion of Heaney's father digging in the garden outside the window. This scene promptly gives way to another, twenty years earlier, of the father digging in potato drills, and then to another of his grandfather, who "cut more turf in a day / Than any other man on Toner's bog." In each case, the activity of digging brings hidden treasures to the surface. The father spades up new potatoes, while the grandfather cuts his way "down and down / For the good turf" (*DN,* 14). The poet finds that although the rhythm and feel and smell of digging inform his existence, he has "no spade to follow men like them." His only choice, then, in answer to this cultural and familial imperative, is to look to the tool at hand: "Between my finger and my thumb / The squat pen rests. / I'll dig with it" (*DN,* 13). This stanza announces, early on, Heaney's predisposition toward circularity or symmetry, repeating as it does the main points of the poem's opening. As the first poem where, by Heaney's own reckoning, "my feelings had got into words" (*P,* 41), "Digging" nevertheless suffers from a too-overt intentionality, explicitly forcing the writing-digging connection, so that the poet himself has subsequently acknowledged its weaknesses, while still claiming the validity of the digging metaphor (*P,* 41–43). That validity establishes itself through its fairly constant recurrence in more successful poems throughout his career.

Even in *Death of a Naturalist* he offers a more subtle reworking of the same idea, through the image in "The Diviner" of the man with the magic talent of witching for water: "The rod jerked down with precise convulsions, / Spring water suddenly broadcasting / Through a green aerial its secret stations" (*DN,* 36). The workings of the diviner are as mysterious as those of the poet, the sensitivity to water as untranslatable into ordinary experience as the sensitivity to the muse. Yet when that inspiration comes, it is unmistakable: the rod's downward twitch is "precise," for the water "broadcasts" its location to him. The process looks so easy that those who watch believe they, too, can master the hazelwood, although, of course, they fail: "It lay dead in their grasp till nonchalantly / He gripped expectant wrists. The hazel stirred." The diviner makes no attempt to explain his art; rather, he simply offers them a glimpse into the magic, taking their wrists and letting them feel the stick's movement. In his essay "Feeling into Words" Heaney lays the poem's genesis back on Sir Philip Sidney's *Apology for Poetry,* which points out the dual meaning of the Latin *vates* as poet and diviner. Moreover, Heaney says, "The diviner resembles the poet in his function of making contact with what lies hidden, and in his ability to make palpable what was sensed or raised (*P,* 48). This poem succeeds in its metaphorical connecting of diviner and poet for precisely the reasons that "Digging" fails. The diviner remains a diviner, not a representative of the poet, and here one is reminded of Pound's dictum that a poem must first of all work for the reader for whom "a hawk is simply a hawk."

In order for the overt analogy to succeed, the poet must not only acknowledge its existence but tease it into something more than a convenient simile. In the book's final poem, "Personal Helicon," Heaney pushes what might have been simply another convenient, homely analogy into something like a personal myth. Dedicated to fellow Northern Irish poet Michael Longley, the poem looks at its outset like another poetry-as-exploring-the-depths poem:

> As a child, they could not keep me from wells
> And old pumps with buckets and windlasses.
> I loved the dark drop, the trapped sky, the smells
> Of waterweed, fungus, and dank moss.
>
> (*DN,* 57)

The attraction, we discover, is largely narcissistic; the young Heaney loved his own reflection. The bulk of the poem offers a recitation of best loved wells and springs and seeps, until we arrive at the present, when it is "beneath all adult dignity" to crawl along the edges of wells, "To stare big-eyed Narcissus." He must find, therefore, some other avenue of self-study, and that avenue is, predictably, poetry: "I rhyme / To see myself, to set the darkness echoing." This attitude has become familiar even at this early stage of his career, yet there is something different about this poem, which Corcoran likens to Theodore Roethke's greenhouse poems, "which similarly elaborate a psychology from a symbolically suggestive childhood world of vegetal processes."[3] Heaney has taken his poem out of the realm of the merely bucolic, has bracketed its meaning through the title. Helicon was the mountain of the muses, its springs a source of poetic inspiration for those who drank from them.

These springs and wells, then, take on a larger meaning from the beginning, so that we are aware of them as both literal and figurative sources of the poem. Heaney engages here in a playful self-referentiality, writing a poem about the creative process that produces it, opening up the mythological possibilities of experience while insisting on their literal description. As the inscription to Longley suggests, this is a poet's poem, and the language ratifies that suspicion. Heaney toys with onomatopoeia, as when the softness of "of ferns and tall / Foxgloves" is surprised by the suddenness of "a rat slapped across my reflection." Hopkinsian, he stacks up stressed syllables, "dragged out long roots," "dark drop," "dank moss," "soft mulch." This is not the language of the Wordsworthian rustic; these lines strut across the page, revelling in their own sound. If Joyce's influence is to be found anywhere in Heaney's verse, it is in the delight the poet takes in the sounds and etymologies of his poems. This poem announces a readiness to move on, to attempt another poetry, even as its final line, with its reference to the darkness, anticipates the subsequent volume.

In this first volume Heaney experiments with, and often stumbles over, tone and diction matters. Particularly troublesome is the poem "Docker," a polemic that misses its mark by several yards. This worker, sitting in the corner of the publichouse, is not man but symbol, not human but mechanical: "The cap juts like a gantry's crossbeam, / Cowling plated forehead and sledgehead jaw. / Speech is clamped in the lips' vice" (*DN,* 41). Not only are the metaphors based on tools, but they are particularly restrictive and violent—the vice, the sledge, the crossbeam that suggests not only a railroad gantry but a gallows. Of course, then, the man's "fist would drop a hammer on a Catholic," for this is a man made of instruments rather than flesh and blood. His "God is a foreman" who will sound the second coming with the "blare" of a "factory horn." We cannot share the poet's scorn at this figure, however real he might be, because he never rises above type; Heaney fails to breathe enough life into him to make us care about or believe in him. As so often happens with this sort of propaganda, the poem turns against the propagandist. When Heaney tells us the "only Roman collar" the Docker will tolerate "Smiles all round his sleek pint of porter," we can only ascribe to the poet the prejudice and intolerance he would place on his character. Ironically, the work proves prophetic, for the Troubles, "that kind of thing," did indeed start again, only two years after the publication of the book. Yet here accuracy loses importance to tone and attitude, and the reader finds it impossible to sympathize with a poem that is capable of so little sympathy of its own.

The chief fault of "Docker," perhaps, is that it wears its feelings too openly. Elsewhere in the volume, Heaney practices the caution, the defensiveness that will characterize much of his later verse. In "Twice Shy" he writes of the reserve that makes courting partners unwilling to speak:

> Our juvenilia
> Had taught us both to wait,
> Not to publish feeling
> And regret it all too late—
> Mushroom loves already
> Had puffed and burst in hate.
> (*DN,* 44)

The mushroom imagery is a delightful device in a poem that otherwise proves quite conventional, even predictable. The mushroom, spontaneous but short-lived, typically does not respond to cultivation, to time and care and nurturing. Its use here suggests an alternative vision of this romance, one more closely based on agricultural experience; the poem, however, leaves that alternative unstated, trusting to the strength of the image to embody its opposite.

His handling of grief is similarly terse and understated in "Mid-Term Break." From the opening the poem seems a recitation of fact: "I sat all morning in the college sick bay / Counting bells knelling classes to a close. / At two o'clock our neighbours drove me home" (*DN,* 28). We have no idea in this first stanza why he sits in the sick bay; not until the first line of stanza 2, when we see the father crying, do we know that the trouble is external. The first and third lines of the opening are conversational and could easily appear in prose.

Throughout the poem Heaney maintains a distance between himself and his material. We can make inferences about his adult feelings only through the precision of his recollection, and the only sensations he reveals of his fourteen-year-old self are of embarrassment and self-consciousness. Indeed, it is the distance that suggests the pain of loss. The ambulance arrives not with a younger brother but with "the corpse." The young Seamus waits until the next morning to see the body, intimating the difficulty involved as well as personal or parental reluctance to open him up to that level of grief just at bedtime. The details he provides instead are of everyone else: his mother's "angry tearless sighs," old men shaking his hand and expressing sorrow, strangers whispering information, and in the midst of it all the baby, who "cooed and laughed and rocked the pram," a happy island untouched by the ocean of sadness surrounding it. Even at the end, when the young Heaney does see the body, the recitation is flat, factual, as he finds his brother "Paler now,"

> Wearing a poppy bruise on his left temple,
> He lay in the four foot box as in his cot.
> No gaudy scars, the bumper knocked him clear.
>
> A four foot box, a foot for every year.
>
> (*DN,* 28)

Clearly this is an unemotional rendering of an emotional moment, and the restraint is not achieved without cost. The regularity of the end-stopped lines, as well as the caesura in the last two lines, suggests the effort involved in suppressing the memory of grief. The verse does not flow; it falters and halts. The final line, despite its heavily alliterative debt to Anglo-Saxon, is heartbreakingly simple, conveying so much more than it says.

In its terseness it recalls a characteristic tone in contemporary British and Irish verse: defensive, tight-lipped, understated. One thinks of a similar hard edge in Jon Silkin's "Death of a Son" or any number of poems by Philip Larkin, Charles Tomlinson, Geoffrey Hill, Roy Fuller, Kavanagh, and Hughes. While the British may have learned that pose and attitude from Thomas Hardy, Edward Thomas and the Georgian poets, as well as, according to Larkin, the privations of World War II, Heaney and the Irish, the Ulster Irish especially, have learned to hold their tongues from extraliterary affairs, particularly matters of local politics, where "whatever you say, you say nothing" (*N*, 59).

Throughout this early volume Heaney reveals his early influences: Gerard Manley Hopkins, Anglo-Saxon verse, Robert Frost, Wordsworth, Yeats, Theodore Roethke, and, of course, Ted Hughes. What he finds among them is a use of nature and farm imagery and subject matter, a readiness to employ the materials at hand, an ability to work successfully in the short lyric and in conventional forms, yet to bend those forms to suit individual vision and whim. Of Hughes's influence on *Death of a Naturalist* much has already been written. Roland Mathias sees the first third of the book, in particular, as "pretty clearly a response to the new climate in poetry initiated by Ted Hughes," a climate of nature and power and life and violence that offers a rough and tumble alternative to the stifling verse of the Movement.[4]

At the same time, however, Mathias also sees Heaney as pulling back from the direct, fascinated gaze Hughes would direct at the natural, nonhuman world. In poems like "The Barn" or "Death of a Naturalist" Heaney shows a child recoiling from nature not because of any inherent threat but because of the overly vigorous workings of his imagination: seeing himself as an interloper from the world of humans, he imagines the nonhuman world preparing a counterattack:

> Right down the dam gross-bellied frogs were cocked
> On sods; their loose necks pulsed like sails. Some hopped:
> The slap and plop were obscene threats. Some sat
> Poised like mud grenades, their blunt heads farting.
> I sickened, turned, and ran. The great slime kings

Were gathered there for vengeance and I knew
That if I dipped my hand the spawn would clutch it.
(*DN,* 16)

In the power of the diction, the explicit violence and sexuality of the imagery, Heaney conveys a young boy's terror at stepping out of his own element into another. Yet the terror is entirely self-manufactured; we know, as does the author, that the frogs are neither vengeful kings nor grenades. Nevertheless, we are likely to recognize (and share in the embarrassment over) the hysterical reaction to an early, direct encounter with nature. This is not a Hughesian poem in sentiment or attitude, yet it may well be in terms of subject matter, imagery, and language.

A poem more conventionally in the Hughes mode is "Trout," which Neil Corcoran identifies as largely unassimilated Hughes, from its elision of title into first line to its "almost absurd range of military metaphors."[5] The trout is "a fat gun-barrel" that "darts like a tracer- / bullet," "A volley of cold blood / / ramrodding the current," who is "fired from the shadows" to the surface, where moths are "torpedoed" (*DN,* 39). Corcoran is correct in asserting, later in the same passage, that in this poem and others, "trout and cow and turkeys disappear unrecognizably into pale imitation and pastiche." The military imagery is more than either the trout or the poem can bear. Throughout this book and the one to follow, Heaney deals more successfully with Hughes's influence in those poems, like "Death of a Naturalist," where he has absorbed that influence, turned it to his own purposes, and filtered it through his own voice.

Certainly the other influences, with the exception of Hopkins (discussed elsewhere in the chapter) are less overt. We may see Roethke peeking out from behind "Churning Day," "Follower," or "Personal Helicon," all with their intimate recall of childhood experience, particularly in the company of adults, yet one suspects Heaney could have found his way into those poems on his own. Similarly, in both title and in the metaphorical use of farm activity, "Blackberry Picking," which he dedicates to his early mentor, Philip Hobsbaum, owes something to Frost's "After Apple Picking"—although we might question whether he found a method in Frost or merely the valorization of a method he would have employed anyway. To find in blackberrying a metaphor for sexual awakening and initiation—and disappointment—is pure Heaney:

> You ate that first one and its flesh was sweet
> Like thickened wine: summer's blood was in it
> Leaving stains upon the tongue and lust for
> Picking.
>
> (*DN,* 20)

The sexual imagery is clear enough, from the sweet flesh to the nearly obscene isolation of "Picking." At the same time, for this is a complex little poem, there is also a more typically Frostian concern with the passing of time and concomitant intimations of mortality. The time is "late August." The fruit, once the first ripened berries appear, comes to fullness quickly, and just as quickly, it spoils, ferments, and, significantly, grows fungus that suggests gray hair. Summer's fruit, like its day, Heaney seems to tell us, hath all too short a lease. Perhaps Frost's influence is seen most clearly not in the poem's thematic concerns but in its cavalier attitude toward its rhyme scheme. Heaney's off-rhymes—"sweet / in it," "ripen / sun," "jam-pots / boots," "covered / burned," "cache / bush," and "peppered / Bluebeard's"—work, as Frost's so often do, to give the poem a conversational air, almost (but not quite) the prose feel of blank verse. There is just enough insistence on rhyme here to maintain the tension between speech and poetry. Elsewhere in the volume Heaney may seem awkward with his rhythms and rhymes, but in "Blackberry Picking" he shows the promise of his later masterful manipulation of prosody.

Door into the Dark

Heaney's second published volume has proven troublesome for critics, since it is neither a clear beginning nor an arrival. Much of the book covers ground very similar to that of *Death of a Naturalist,* while there are also intimations, rarely entirely successful in themselves, of the directions his verse will take in subsequent books. That combination makes for an unsatisfactory, at times frustrating, reading experience. While there are a number of remarkable poems in the volume, as a whole it has neither the delight of the new one finds in *Death of a Naturalist* nor the visceral and intellectual impact of *North.*

Heaney, ever careful about the structuring of his books, picks up a number of threads from his first work: themes, subjects, images, rhythms. The most obvious connection between the two books appears in the title. Heaney ends "Personal Helicon," a poem in which he revels in finding his image in the "dark drop" of old wells, by saying he rhymes "To see myself, to set the darkness echoing" (*DN*, 57). When the title phrase of the second book opens "The Forge," we are not surprised that this poem, like "Personal Helicon," deals metaphorically with the act of poetic creation.

In this poem, however, Heaney situates the speaker in the position of the reader, the outsider excluded from the creative mystery:

> All I know is a door into the dark.
> Outside, old axles and iron hoops rusting;
> Inside, the hammered anvil's short-pitched ring,
> The unpredictable fantail of sparks
> Or hiss when a new shoe toughens in water.
> The anvil must be somewhere in the centre,
> Horned as a unicorn, at one end square,
> Set there immoveable: an altar
> Where he expends himself in shape and music.
> Sometimes, leather-aproned, hairs in his nose,
> He leans out on the jamb, recalls a clatter
> Of hoofs where traffic is flashing in rows;
> Then grunts and goes in, with a slam and a flick
> To beat real iron out, to work the bellows.[6]

I reprint this poem in its entirety both because the sonnet's length permits quoting whole and because the poem is so tightly knit, so thoroughly of a piece that to excerpt is to damage irreparably. In his essay "Feeling into Words" Heaney distinguishes technique, which puts a personal stamp of style and voice and vision into poetry, from mere craft, which he identifies as "the skill of making" (*P*, 47), and he singles out for praise Patrick Kavanagh, whose craft often faltered but whose technique was sound. Yet in this poem as in others of the early period, he celebrates precisely that "skill of making," in the craft of the blacksmith as, elsewhere, that of the diviner or the thatcher or the digger. To the outsider, at least (and perhaps to the young Heaney as well), the most obvious attribute of art is craft.

The speaker of the poem finds himself shut out of the process of creation inside the smithy. He can see the objects sitting outside waiting for repair, yet the world inside is closed to him "with a slam and a flick," leaving him reliant on inferences he can draw from sounds and glimpses. The anvil's ring, the shoe's hiss in water, the marvelously realized "unpredictable fantail of sparks" fail to convey fully the smith's world or his process of making. When Neil Corcoran complains that "the real occupation tends to disappear behind its metaphorical significance,"[7] he misses the premise and movement of the poem, which is not about being a blacksmith; rather, it is precisely about *not* being a blacksmith. The misreading has serious implications: if one views the subject as the blacksmith's craft, then Corcoran's objections—the absence of any real presence of the smith, the sentimentality of the presentation, even the "strained religious metaphor" that equates the anvil with an altar—all stand up. If, however, one understands the poem's subject as the inaccessibility of artistic mystery to the nonartist (and the failure of the bystanders in "The Diviner" supports such a reading) then there is a logic driving these alleged "weaknesses." The speaker is not intimate with either the smith, who appears only occasionally at the door, or with the apparently secret skills of his trade.

Beyond those sketchy clues that reach the street, the reality of the smithy remains past reach, behind the "door into the dark." The mystery leads to mystification and to awe. The anvil, unseen, "must be somewhere in the centre," although the speaker can only speculate. Hidden from view as it is, the anvil takes on magical and elusive properties, becomes "horned as a unicorn," then transforms into an altar, the smith himself becoming the priest of a lost religion. He clings tightly, inarticulately to the past. Romantic Ireland may be, as Yeats asserts, dead and gone, but, Heaney suggests in this and a number of other early poems, it is not quite forgotten. Elevated to what Robert Buttel calls a " 'leather-aproned' Hephaestus,"[8] the smith inspires wonder in the speaker akin to our wonder at the poet's ability to create the poem, "To beat real iron out, to work the bellows." Where the diviner in the earlier poem shows but does not explain his art to the bystanders, the smith refuses even that contact, evidently content in his creative solitude. All of this, of course, is not to deny the poem's faults: the lameness of "hairs in his nose" (intended, apparently, to lend a reality to the smith, while actually violating the distance the poem otherwise maintains between speaker and craftsman), the irregularity of the rhyme scheme in the sestet and indeed in the second couplet. Still, the poem is a marvelous wall of sound; we meet the poet at *his* leather-aproned, sweat-stained, muscular best in a sonnet that is much more subtle and cagey than its critics might have us believe.

Another thread Heaney picks up from the first book and develops further in *Door into the Dark* is the problem of land and sea defining one another. Here again he demonstrates progression in his thinking. Whereas in "Lovers on Aran" the questions posed by the shore remained strictly in the realm of a lovers' relationship, in "The Peninsula" and, to a greater extent, "Shoreline" politics and history begin to exert their influence over the poet. "The Peninsula" is an insistently solitary poem, admonishing the reader in its first line to drive around the peninsula all day "When you have nothing more to say" (*DD,* 21). The poem builds upon that initial sense of isolation, describing "The land without marks so you will not arrive / But pass through." An arrival would entail a possibility of contact, of communication, while the purpose of this drive remains, beginning to end, to deny contact. When, at dusk, horizon and ploughed field seem to consume features of the landscape, it seems desirable that "you're in the dark again." Quite appropriately, then, this poem contains back-to-back examples of that peculiarly inward-turned figure that Christopher Ricks, in *The Force of Poetry,* calls "the self-infolded simile."[9] Although he uses it specifically in conjunction with the poetry of Andrew Marvell, he also notes it in the work of recent Ulster poets, including Heaney, who in this poem presents the reader with a double: "The leggy birds stilted on their own legs, / Islands riding themselves out into the fog." Although in one case the figure borders on tautology—of course birds are stilted on their own legs—and in the other on logical impossibility, in both cases they succeed because they reinforce the sense of isolation at work in the poem: look here, they seem to say, even metaphors have nowhere to turn but inward.

When the reader arrives home again, it is "still with nothing to say" "Except that now you will uncode all landscapes / By this: things founded clean on their own shapes, / Water and ground in their extremity." The phrase "all landscapes" is well placed, for it suggests to us, as perhaps the only hint in the poem, political landscapes as well. The emphasis on the rough boundary line of hostile elements suggests, certainly in retrospect, the jagged boundary of alien social elements as well. While such consideration may not be the main thrust of the poem, the engulfing "all," the island image, and the social extremity suggested by having nothing more to say would seem to support a social reading, whether the terms are Ulster and the Republic, Protestant and Catholic, or a more intimate pairing. The poem's tension resides to a large degree in the interplay between the turning inward and the outward encounter.

The poet's fascination with the meeting of land and sea manifests itself again in "Shoreline": "there's the sea / Sidling and settling to / The back of a hedge," a tide coming in "At the foot of all fields, / All cliffs and shingles" (*DD,* 51). The verbs suggest an intimacy between water and earth not seen in the previous poem: "sidling and settling," "rummaging," "froth." This is a much cozier poem than "The Peninsula," yet also more explicitly threatening. Danger has traditionally come to Ireland from the sea, and in this poem the very sound of the sea carries that peril:

> Listen. Is it the Danes,
> A black hawk bent on the sail?
> Or the chinking Normans?
> Or currachs hopping high
>
> On to the sand?
>
> (*DD,* 52)

This poem makes explicit what elsewhere is implicit in Heaney's diction: life in Northern Ireland is filled with evidence of the successive waves of invaders, so much so that the very air and sea carry their sounds. There is much left to refine, of course. Later, the currachs, the boats carrying, presumably, the Scots-English planters (the word itself is Gaelic and common to both Scotland and Ireland), will take on more threatening, often specifically sexual qualities. Shedding light on current affairs can wait for another poem. "Shoreline" advocates the poet's later manner, even beginning to employ what Philip Hobsbaum identifies as the "loose quatrain" that Heaney learned chiefly from Patrick Kavanagh, although here he has not quite mastered it.[10]

Although he never quite finds success in the loose quatrain form, he dabbles in it throughout the last half of *Door into the Dark,* especially in the final poems: "Whinlands," "The Plantation," "Shoreline," "Bann Clay," and "Bogland." Significantly, they all work in the same territory: piercing through to the past, finding connections to modern society. "Whinlands" offers a particularly striking example. Although the poem operates on a metaphorical level, suggesting that whins—*gorse* in England—present an analog to Irish society, such a level operates only very late in the poem, perhaps only in the final stanza. The first three stanzas are strictly descriptive. Only in the fourth stanza does Heaney offer a clue that something else might be at work, when, in describing their highly inflammable nature, he writes that whins burn not with a visible flame in daytime but with "a fierce heat tremor"

(*DD,* 47). The use of "fierce" attributes a human quality to this otherwise natural phenomenon, although by itself it remains merely interesting. Similarly, when the ensuing stanza asserts that the fire takes only the thorns but not the woody stems, which "Remain like bone, charred horn," the line intrigues but does not resolve.

Not until the final stanza does the poet play his hand:

> Gilt, jaggy, springy, frilled
> This stunted, dry richness
> Persists on hills, near stone ditches,
> Over flintbeds and battlefields.
> (*DD,* 48)

Like Irish life, one might add. This is Heaney exercising the flash and spark of his mature style. The first line, with its Old English roots in the first three words, forces the reader's attention toward language itself as analogous to the whins: a richness grown up over the leavings of history. Indeed, the entire stanza is a marvel of language, from the absolute economy to the oxymoron of "stunted . . . richness" to the near-total consonance and reversal of sounds in "*fl*in*tbeds–battle*f*ie*l*ds.*" This final stanza leads the reader back through the poem to a consideration of Northern Irish society, perhaps all society—insistent, thorny, volatile, tenacious—being founded on this same base of largely forgotten or hidden history or prehistory.

Clearly, the pull of history is growing stronger for Heaney in his second book. When the volume arrives at "Bogland," then, Heaney seems to find what he has been searching for throughout the book: a natural place that is also the repository of history. The bogs can yield up treasures greater than coal, forgotten or lost parts of a heritage, butter "recovered salty and white" after a hundred years, or the skeleton of the Great Irish Elk, long since extinct. These treasures appear as the modern investigators dig back toward the spot of origin, despite the knowledge that "The wet centre is bottomless." While Heaney has not yet discovered the true riches the bogs can hold for him as poet, "Bogland" demonstrates a remarkable prescience of the future direction of his verse.

There is a circularity to the movement of the poem—or, rather, described in the poem—that characterizes the volume as a whole. A celebration of the natural cycle of eels and their fishermen (to whom the poem is dedicated), "A Lough Neagh Sequence" builds upon images of circularity. From the repetition of the first line, "The lough will claim a victim every year," in the last line of the opening poem, "Up the Shore," the sequence carries frequent reminders that the life it describes follows rhythms of cycle and return. In "Setting," the fourth poem, the line with hooks lies "coiled in the stern," while "The oars in their locks go round and round," and when the remains of the bait are tossed away, "The gulls encompass them before the water." Throughout the poems there are references to garlands and compasses and circularity, which reach their ultimate expression in the fifth poem, "Lifting." There, after describing the eels weaving themselves into a continuous "knot of back and pewter belly" (*DD,* 42), Heaney sees the fishermen similarly enwound by each other, their wakes interweaving one with another, asking: "And when did this begin? / This morning, last year, when the lough first spawned? / The crews will answer, 'Once the season's in' " (*DD,* 43). The fishermen, as much a part of the cycle as the eels they catch, display the lack of recognition of pattern characteristic of Wordsworth's rustic. For them every day is new, every season a separate experience. Like the eels, too, they travel the straight line that brings them full circle, as Heaney expresses it in "The Plantation."

The sequence also stands as an advance in Heaney's approach to politics in his verse. The issue of politics, or of the Catholic minority versus the British authority or the Protestant majority, never arises; the poems, particularly the first, clearly sympathize with the traditional Irish (and, by implication, Catholic and even nationalist) way of life. Heaney dedicates the poem "for the fishermen," which seems simple enough, yet the fishermen are technically violating the law. In place of official rights Heaney posits natural, historical rights. The British company violates the natural cycle of the eel by setting up weirs and sluice-gates at Toomebridge, where they "lift five hundred stone in one go." By contrast, the fishermen operate on a sense of fair play, which makes them "confront them one by one / And sail miles out, and never learn to swim." When questioned on the wisdom of not learning to swim, they fall back on fatalism and a sense of natural, even cosmic rightness: "We'll be quicker going down," they explain, believing that no matter what, "The lough will claim a victim every year." The poet's sympathy for the fishermen's position and attitudes is in itself a political statement; he need not push beyond that.

Political and historical concerns manifest themselves elsewhere in *Door into the Dark,* notably in "Requiem for the Croppies," in which all nature, seemingly, sides with the rebels, who are ultimately overcome by superior, and foreign, technology. The narrator, speaking from beyond the grave, situates them initially within an agrarian context, their pockets filled with barley, since they had no time or facilities for cooking. Using the farm landscape to advantage, they would "stampede cattle into infantry / Then retreat through hedges where cavalry must be thrown" (*DD,* 24). The rebellion of 1798, however, did not end in victory, but in the terrible slaughter on Vinegar Hill, where

> Terraced thousands died, shaking scythes at cannon.
> The hillside blushed, soaked in our broken wave.
> They buried us without shroud or coffin
> And in August the barley grew up out of the grave.
> (*DD,* 24)

Here again, nature conspires with the native Irish, the hill blushing with the blood of the massacred, the barley a silent witness to the slaughter. Yet the barley is more than that; it also points to a harvest of further rebellion, so that the battle at Vinegar Hill becomes the seed of the Easter 1916 uprising and, ultimately, of Irish independence. We know now, of course, as did Heaney when he published the book in 1969, that those seeds had not all grown to fullness. Perhaps, however, even he was surprised at how soon a new harvest would begin.

Chapter Three

Growing to Maturity: *Wintering Out* and *Stations*

In 1917 William Butler Yeats discovered, or was discovered by (agency here is difficult to establish), a coherent mythology, a system of symbols for his subsequent work. The spirit world spoke through his wife's automatic writing, or at least he believed it did, and the resulting visionary material supplied him with poetic symbols for the rest of his career: interpenetrating gyres, towers, and winding stairs—the Great Wheel of history in which new ages are ushered in by the annunciation of the gods to men.

Such large-scale gifts of informing principles rarely occur; the great mass of poets struggles along piecing together elements of personal mythology without ever receiving a massive infusion of inspiration (a word that is very much suspect in modern culture). Still, occasionally something that no other word in the language seems to describe so well will grace a poet's career and offer him the possibility of bringing unity (another Yeatsian word) to his poetry. Such an event occurred in 1969 when Seamus Heaney discovered P. V. Glob's *The Bog People.*

Glob's book presents the fascinating discoveries of bodies in Jutland, some of them nearly two thousand years old, of victims of civil executions and ritual sacrifices whose deaths included partial or total stripping, throat slashing, and being dumped into the bogs. The bodies, along with some articles of clothing such as leather belts and caps and the bonds that held them at the time of death, have been preserved by the tannin in the bogs; their effect on the modern observer is eerily magnetic. For Heaney, who in his early poems had often pictured the earth in general and bogs in particular as the storeroom of history, and who had used the digging metaphor so frequently in his work, the discovery of Glob's book suddenly offered him symbols, ready-made and ideal for the task, to unify his entire vision. In the hanged, maimed, and drowned bodies pictured in *The Bog People,* Heaney finds the symbols for neighborly treachery, vengeance, and destruction in modern Northern Ireland.

From the beginning of his career, as we have seen, Heaney has been interested in poetry as a kind of digging; the metaphor attracts him for several reasons, chief among them that his sense of place focuses his attention on digging as a central activity in the lives of the local people. They dig their fuel, their food, their graves. In both his first two works, Heaney frequently turns his attention to the act of digging and to the act of writing as a corollary, but he fails to find the goal of all that turning of sod. Occasionally he comes close, as when he describes the potato harvest as a ritual that

> Recurs mindlessly as autumn. Centuries
> Of fear and homage to the famine god
> Toughen the muscles behind humbled knees,
> Make a seasonal altar of the sod.
> (*DN*, 31)

Many of these early poems are quite good in themselves, but as a body they lack the resonance that marks the mature work of a master poet.

Then Heaney experienced the fortuitous coincidence that we would reject as forced in a work of fiction. He closed his second volume with "Bogland," in which he marvels at the preservative qualities of Irish bogs where butter keeps fresh for centuries and coal will never form. Later in the same year, 1969, he found Glob, and realized that his mistake had been in looking at the wrong bogs. Irish bogs held many wonders and were personally and locally interesting, with their skeletons of the Great Irish Elk, but the symbols Heaney really needed were being excavated in Jutland.

His third volume, *Wintering Out* (1972), contains the first of his poems about the bog people, "The Tollund Man," about the victim of ritual sacrifice to the fertility goddess. Heaney is explicit about the connection in his own mind between that sacrifice and some that are closer to home:

> Taken in relation to the tradition of Irish political martyrdom . . . this is more than an archaic barbarous rite: it is an archetypal pattern. And the unforgettable photographs of these victims blended in my mind with photographs of atrocities, past and present, in the long rites of Irish political and religious struggles. (*P*, 57–58)

The blending also makes its way into the poem itself:

> I could risk blasphemy,
> Consecrate the cauldron bog
> Our holy ground and pray
> Him to make germinate
>
> The scattered, ambushed
> Flesh of labourers,
> Stockinged corpses
> Laid out in farmyards,
>
> Tell-tale skin and teeth
> Flecking the sleepers
> Of four young brothers, trailed
> For miles along the lines.[1]

The sudden coincidence of discovery and necessity blends the image of the Tollund man into a powerful symbol of men sacrificed to inscrutable forces and to the community's needs, and turns the poet's statement around: the atrocities, past and present, become not merely modern barbarities but modern versions of an archetypal pattern.

That he sees the Tollund man within a larger framework of sacrifice is made obvious in the connection to both the current reference to the four young brothers and to the 1798 slaughter of the Croppies, from whose pockets, as he tells us in "Requiem for the Croppies," the barley they carried sprouted in August. What he cannot see, however, is the renewal that may grow out of the contemporary violence. While it may indeed follow that modern sacrifice may engender the movement symbolized by Kathleen ni Houlihan, the dream of a unified Irish Republic, the poem refuses to make that leap. The reference echoes something of Eliot's fear of sterility in *The Waste Land,* in which the poet asks, ironically, regarding the corpse buried in the garden, whether it has sprouted yet. In each case, the poet fears that the fertility ritual may fail, may not even apply, in the modern world.

While the poem does not follow Eliot's masterpiece in other respects, there is a corollary movement in looking beyond the boundaries of the immediate society for a working mythology that will enable the poet to understand and interpret that society. If the Tollund man is joined with not the mistress of Irish republicanism but with the Norse goddess of fertility, he is nevertheless transported out of this life in a fatal, clearly sexual, embrace:

> She tightened her torc on him
> And opened her fen,
> Those dark juices working
> Him to a saint's kept body . . .
> (*WO,* 47)

Clearly, this fertilty myth is much darker than that of, say, Osiris, in which the priestess of Isis took human lovers as surrogates for the dismembered god. The short companion poem, which Heaney also pairs with this one in his *Selected Poems,* entitled "Nerthus" after the goddess, reinforces the sexuality of the ritual, with its description of a forked ash stick, "Its long grains gathering to the gouged split" (*WO,* 49). Both the "gouged split" and the opening of the fen are suggestive of female genitalia, thereby making explicit the specifically sexual nature of the entry of the male body into the bog.

Yet there is something more going on here than simply recalling an archaic ritual. The bog's juices are "dark," hinting at not only vaginal secretions (which themselves remain hidden, dark) but at a deeper mystery behind that surface level of meaning. The waters of the fen do not devour their victim; rather, they turn his form into a "saint's kept body." This pre-Christian pattern flows into a Christian, specifically Catholic, form of belief: his body, turned into a relic of worship (Heaney promises to make a pilgrimage to Aarhus to see the corpse), becomes holy because his sacrifice, like that of the Christian saints, was for the causes of belief and community. Implicit in that connection is the question of the saintliness of more recent sacrifices. In the final third of the poem, Heaney discovers a sense of kinship with the people of Jutland, another Northern race, despite the strangeness of language and custom:

> Out there in Jutland
> In the old man-killing parishes
> I will feel lost,
> Unhappy and at home.
> (*WO,* 48)

Again the local reference sneaks into the discussion through the word "parish," which, like the saints mentioned earlier, introduces a Catholic element into the poem. He will feel at home, one may surmise, because the six counties of Ulster have become the new man-killing parishes. The poet finds in the Tollund man, in the bog people generally, a visual and historical analog to the current Troubles.

While this discovery does not translate into a controlling metaphor for the book—that must wait until *North*—scattered throughout *Wintering Out* is evidence of a new approach to poetry, a heightened sensitivity to the historical and political implications of many of Heaney's interests and preoccupations. The emphasis on land and digging, for instance, remains, although it yields up new insights. The Tollund man, Heaney notes, was discovered by turf cutters, who have moved from simply being a personal point of reference in "Digging" to offering a perspective from which past and present may be observed.

One of the outgrowths of that sense of perspective is the interest in language in the book. "The Wool Trade," with a Stephen Dedalus revery on pronunciation as its epigraph, concentrates attention on the sounds of language, the texture of words like the texture of cloth. The poem is a kaleidoscope of vowel sounds, in particular, with a line like "To shear, to bale and bleach and card" (*WO,* 37) calling attention not only to the possibilities of play among vowels but to pronunciation differences between dialect groups. These differences highlight cultural, religious, and political distinctions with which the Northern Irish must contend: the merchant class, those who would go to the Netherlands and trade with men with "soft names like Bruges," were Scots-Anglo-Irish Protestants, those who raised the sheep and spun the wool and wove the cloth likely to be "native" Catholics. The sounds "hang" to be examined, studied, even admired in "the gallery of the tongue." Throughout the volume he emphasizes speech patterns and, as Blake Morrison notes, images of the tongue: "the river tongues" in "A New Song," "the swinging tongue" of Henry Joy McCracken's body in "Linen Town," "the slab of the tongue" in "Toome," "the civil tongues" of "The Last Mummer."[2] The poet's position in all this proliferation of speech, then, must necessarily be that of listener, and Heaney also presents numerous images of himself listening. If he will but keep his ear in "this loop of silence" long enough, he says in "Land," he will eventually pick up "a small drumming" (*WO,* 22). In "Gifts of Rain" he speaks of a man who "fords / his life by soundings" (*WO,* 23), and then repeats the word "Soundings" by itself, for emphasis. In "Oracle" he connects the two functions of speech and hearing, "small mouth and ear / in a woody cleft" (*WO,* 28).

And, of course, throughout the work he actively listens for the sounds of words, especially of place names. The first of the place-name poems, "Anahorish," also stands logically first in the poet's experience. As Heaney explains in a 1972 *Guardian* article, the word is an Anglicization of *anach fhior uisce,* "the place of clear water," while the place was a townland that bordered the family farm, Mossbawn, as well as the school he attended until age twelve (*P,* 36). This poem offers more, however, than mere local color or personal reminiscence, although this element does occupy the first third, offering him a way into the verse. It is the sound itself, however, that occupies the thematic as well as physical center of the poem, "soft gradient / of consonant, vowel meadow" (*WO,* 16), which leads him in turn to first a contemporary image of "lamps / swung through the yards / on winter evenings" and then to something much older, where

> those mound-dwellers
> go waist-deep in mist
> to break the light ice
> at wells and dunghills.
> (*WO,* 16)

While "mound-dwellers" can refer simply to the presence of the hill in the townland of Anahorish, it also recalls a lost time, before the successive invasions of Romans, Vikings, and Englishmen, a time that is itself "waist-deep in mist," when Gaelic was the mother tongue. The sounds of this poem reinforce the softness of "Anahorish": the softer consonants, *m, n, l, r,* and *s,* predominate in a self-conscious departure from the harder verse inspired by Old English and Hopkins he has already favored in his early books and to which he will return in *North.*

The tension involved in language and the history words carry with them feature prominently in another of the two place-name poems in the volume "Toome": "My mouth holds round / the soft blastings, / *Toome, Toome*" (*WO,* 26). The physical sensation of a word, although our first contact with it, remains unexamined for most people and most words. *Toome,* on the other hand, is a special place and a special sound, therefore calling for Heaney's attention. Located in the Bann valley, about which he has already written in "Bann Clay," Toome is both the site of archaeological finds and of the rebellion of 1798, an event that greatly occupies the poet's thinking in the period immediately after the unrest of 1969. In this case the sound of the name instigates a turning back on language itself, a looking under "the slab of the tongue," the immediacies of daily usage, to a discovery of the treasures housed in the "souterrain," the underground chamber or storehouse, of linguistic memory. Heaney finds a highly mixed cache, both the items of ordinary life—jewelry (torcs) and kitchen leavings—and the evidence of the violent, military past of the island, the flints and musketballs. This poem, yielding historical perspective from musings on language, marks a shift from the digging poems of his earlier work, whether of the local color stripe like "Digging" or the archaeological stripe of "Bann Clay" or "Bogland." Here, he realizes the possibilities of his poetry as an instrument of linguistic excavation, thereby fulfilling the promise made in "Digging." In method, attitude, imagery, and style—the quatrains that Philip Hobsbaum complains are too fixed, too preset, unlike the loose quatrains of Patrick Kavanagh[3]—Heaney has moved much closer to the poetics of *North.* Indeed, some of the criticism Hobsbam addresses to the stanzaic form here is a product of a transitional mode: Heaney only rarely achieves the kind of power within the limited space of the short-line quatrains in *Wintering Out* that he routinely manages in the subsequent book.

The issue of language use—what one speaks and how one speaks it—appears in a variety of poems in the volume. In "Traditions" Heaney sets up the opposition, to which he adheres in later work, between masculine, rapacious England and feminine, ravished Ireland. The Irish "gutteral muse," he says, was long since "bulled," the term charged with sexual violence and massive, brute force, by England's "alliterative tradition," a reference to the alliterative poetics of Old English and early Middle English verse. Tradition, he further notes, repeats the violation and "beds us down into / the British isles" (*WO,* 31). Ireland, no matter how she may protest, cannot escape the conspiracy of geography and custom. Here the reference gains impact from Heaney's subsequent career, for in the 1983 pamphlet *An Open Letter,* he energetically, if humorously, objects to being included in an anthology of *British* verse, noting, among other things, "the name's not right."[4] Later, after noting evidence of the Elizabethan invasion—diction, archaisms, references to Shakespeare's *Henry V* and Spenser's *State of Ireland*—and of lowland Scots words "bawn" and "mossland" (a canny use of his childhood residence), he cites Leopold Bloom, who responds to the question of nationality "sensibly," in *Ulysses:* " 'Ireland,' said Bloom, 'I was born here. Ireland.' " Bloom, of course, is the ultimate outsider, a Jew of Hungarian ancestry with no claim to native status, no connection to

Irish heritage or language. He speaks in English, naturally, as does everyone else in the novel, as does Heaney, and this is the point: however much one may feel the ignominy of speaking the conquerors' language, English is not merely the mother tongue but the *native* tongue of modern Ireland, just as the English literary tradition also forms, like it or not, a major part of the Irish literary landscape. The facts may prove distasteful; they are, nevertheless, undeniable.

In fact, in the preceding poem, "The Backward Look," Heaney has already elegized the long-dead Irish tongue. The poem's ostensible subject is the flight of the snipe, whose elusive, darting path is

> A stagger in the air
> as if a language
> failed, a sleight
> of wing.
> (*WO,* 29)

This stanza is itself elusive, abruptly shifting, with its declining *6-5-3-2* syllabic pattern and the caesura in the extremely short third line, which breaks all forward momentum even as it turns the figure from linguistic exhaustion to magic. The sound of the stanza, not surprisingly, with its repetition of *g* and *l,* the terminal consonants in "gutteral," Heaney's favorite word for describing Gaelic ("our gutteral muse," he says), further calls to mind the pastness of the language. The diction of the stanza indicates once more the growth of his poetry as it moves toward the method of *North,* with its heavy reliance on Old English or Old Norse roots. No longer is he merely playing with words; rather, he is dredging up the past through them, exploring the ways in which one language may elide into another, in which a modern tongue carries its nonlinguistic historical baggage.

The second stanza, however, calls into question which language has failed, as the snipe flees "into dialect, into variants." The remnants of the language have indeed made their way into the Irish dialects of English (as well as into American and other dialects), yet English itself follows the pattern of languages to grow and change and break up into dialects that threaten to become independent.

The elusive quality of the trickster, the snipe, suggests that even if English is the language under discussion, it is nevertheless the dialect that replaced the native Irish Gaelic rather than the one spoken by descendants of the Planters. This is a peculiarly Irish bird Heaney describes (and here it is well to remember the local reference to the snipe in "Dawn Shoot"), whose "tail-feathers" drum

> elegies
> in the slipstream
>
> of wild goose
> and yellow bittern
> as he corkscrews away.
> (*WO*, 29)

These are not the noble birds of Yeats's "Wild Swans at Coole," but much homier fowl; Heaney is not pining over the fading ideal of an Augustan society but memorializing the loss of national identity as evidenced by the passing of the Irish language. The key phrase in the above passage is "wild goose," recalling as it does the tradition, dating back to the uprising of 1798, of Irish rebels fleeing the country, often to fight as mercenaries in foreign armies. As they flee, of course, they take their language with them, dispersing words and phrases where they land.

Even the flight of the snipe follows a very Irish course, over "earthworks / and wall-steads" and, in a brilliant dovetailing of meanings, "through the sniper's eyrie," the original, natural being giving way to another familiar, although political and highly menacing, figure. The poet's bringing together of these two common, related words points to a secondary connection: the political prisoners in places like Maze prison, as well as the provisional wing of the Irish Republican Army and some elements of the broader nationalist movement, have embraced the Irish language, insisting in some instances on conducting their business in it. This highly charged political gesture, although doomed to failure, signals rebellious intent and anti-English sentiment. Yet the poem also signals the innate futility of such a gesture, for the snipe remains elusive:

> disappearing among
> gleanings and leavings
> in the combs
> of a fieldworker's archive.
> (*WO*, 30)

The prospect of reviving Irish Gaelic will probably remain attractive to successive generations of nationalists, just as it was in Yeats's time, yet the attraction is based on nostalgia, not pragmatism. The language is gone, as Heaney further reminds the reader with the image of the extinct wolf and the degraded wolfhound in "Midnight," surviving only as remnants in the Irish dialect of English and in textbooks, and no effort, no matter how Herculean, can revive a dead language. The book itself is a testament to the triumph of English.

Even in poems not specifically about language, the issues involved in English use arise. In "The Other Side," for example, the neighbor's speech is "that tongue of chosen people" (*WO,* 34). The neighbor stands at the stream's edge, surveying the Heaneys' property, and his pronouncement, "It's poor as Lazarus, that ground," stands as a judgment on not a single farm run by one Catholic family, but on the entire Northern Irish minority. In part 2 the man, in the midst of a religious discussion, notes that Catholics, in sharp contradistinction to his Presbyterian people, "hardly rule by the book at all." The heavy reliance on direct, personal reading of the Bible among Protestant sects becomes an identifying feature: "His brain was a whitewashed kitchen / hung with texts, swept tidy / as the body o' the kirk" (*WO,* 35). That final line further distances neighbor from neighbor, with its Norse-derived Scots "kirk," a word a Catholic would never apply to his church. The orderliness, moreover, of the man's mind stands in contrast to the Heaneys' way of life, with its fallow ground, its "moss and rushes," its muttered litanies. Indeed, in part 3, the man hesitates in deference to rosaries being said in the kitchen before knocking at the door.

Clearly, he, too, feels himself an outsider, and it is at that level that the poet, who has been in some danger of reducing the man to a cultural stereotype, finds common ground. In the "now" of the poem, a time of family grief, the man stands "in the dark yard" (*WO,* 36), tapping his blackthorn "shyly, as if he were party to / lovemaking of a stranger's weeping." And in a sense, of course, it is a stranger's grief, for he never knows his neighbors any more than they know him. His uncertainty, so unlike his earlier assured pronoucements, his uneasiness, brings Heaney to his own dilemma:

> Should I slip away, I wonder,
> or go up and touch his shoulder
> and talk about the weather
>
> or the price of grass-seed?
>
> (*WO,* 36)

The first fact about this man, after all, is not that he is a Protestant, but that he is a neighbor. It is the second fact, with all its attendant complications, that interferes with interactions that both speaker and subject would maintain on the basis of the first. We are social beings, and one of our basic drives is to accommodate ourselves to accidents of geography; though the occupant of the next farm or the next quarter acre be a member of a group we mistrust, our initial instinct and desire is to maintain civility. Intercourse between the two in this poem takes place not in the rhetoric of the Paisleyite or the Provos, but in the language of the commonplace, weather and grass seed, safe trivialities.

The poet's sensibility struggles within itself to the point of paralysis, ultimately desiring to do the right thing while being unable to discern what the right thing might be; entertaining simultaneously the urge to withdraw and the urge to act. That romantic removal of the poet from the realm of praxis, which Anne Stevenson in her essay on *Stations* traces in a line from Wordsworth by way of Joyce and Kavanagh, is a position we have seen before in his work and one which will occupy a greater place in the books that follow *Wintering Out.*[5] Here, though, it is complicated by a host of contradictory feelings, chief among them the polarities that this man, who is so very other, so alien, remains all the while a fellow Irishman. The book carries other such reminders. The lone member of the rebellion of 1798 mentioned by name in the book is Henry Joy McCracken, executed in Belfast for his role as leader of a Protestant uprising in County Antrim well after the main rebellion had been quashed. Heaney's sensitivity to the common ground between his side and "the other side" effectively prevents him from wholeheartedly taking sides, despite Paisley-run *Protestant Telegraph*'s characterization of him as a "well-known papist propagandist." If Heaney's sentiments are firmly with the minority, he nevertheless recognizes that Protestant and Catholic alike are victims of historical circumstance.

These political and linguistic concerns, while they occupy a majority of the book, do not comprise the entirety of it. *Wintering Out* contains a second part, which, if the first anticipates *North,* looks even further ahead, to *Field Work.* The more personal and immediate concerns of part 2 reflect a continuing, if largely heretofore undeveloped, aspect of his work. Heaney's forays into love poetry have been brief and not altogether successful. Throughout his early books, his voice lends itself most readily to uneasiness, anguish, unpleasantness; the transition to happiness, satisfaction, or love pledges occasionally becomes too great a leap.

The personal poems of *Wintering Out,* however, are themselves tinged with sadness and edginess. "Wedding Day" begins with the flat statement, "I am afraid" (*WO,* 57). The speaker here, the groom, finds himself totally disoriented on a day when "Sound has stopped" and "images reel." The day, usually associated with boundless happiness and optimism, seems filled with loss: the father's "wild grief," the guests filled with "mourning," the new wife sings beside the cake "Like a deserted bride," a figure he elaborates after the figure of Dickens's Miss Havisham. Only the commonplace figure of a heart with an arrow through it on the men's room wall redeems the day, reminds the speaker of his love and of the promise as well as the closure the day holds, permits him to ask to "Sleep on your breast to the airport." Any man or woman who has ever gone through a wedding day will probably recognize the uncertainty brought on by the sense of something ending, whether or not one accepts the poem's hyperbole.

Throughout part 2 Heaney emphasizes loss and ending, but on a much more personal, immediate scale than in part 1. The mermaid-charmed woman-suicide of "Maighdean Mara" has her "magic garment" stolen; the "Bye-Child" has been robbed of the power of speech by the horrors of parental abuse; the runaway daughter of "A Winter's Tale" (her running away itself an emblem of loss) is mad; the mother in "Limbo" drowns her child; the "Shore Woman" walks the strand, resentful of her husband's crudity and the failure of love between them.

Yet perhaps the most painful and revealing, because most fully felt, poem in part 2 is "Summer Home." The poem's setting and movement suggest a parallel with the Heaneys' summer in Spain in 1969; whether or not the piece is autobiographical, however, it beautifully realizes the condition of "summer gone sour" (*WO,* 59), of a troubled relationship. In the first section, a host of images conspire to articulate the marital difficulties the speaker and his wife experience. The breeze blows in "off the dumps," and either that or the heat speaks to them of the soured summer, or "a fouled nest incubating somewhere." Further on, a mat is "larval" with insects, requiring a harshly purifying alternative, "scald, scald, scald." Through all this unpleasantness, the speaker turns "inquisitor," attempting to determine "whose fault" the rift may be. One would be hard pressed to find ten lines of poetry more hostile to human habitation than this personal wasteland.

The remainder of the poem struggles mightily not to give in to the fetid atmosphere of the first section. In the second, the speaker, accepting the blame as he bedecks the door with "wild cherry and rhododendron," an "unlikely Proserpine," as Corcoran calls him.[6] When the flower petals "taint to a sweet chrism" (*WO,* 60), he asks his wife to "Attend. Annoint the wound." The sacramental nature of both this last line and the word "chrism" point to a renewal, or at least a wish for renewal, of the marital sacrament, as well as a ritual healing of the "wound" in the relationship. The poem struggles throughout with the war between wishes and reality, between what could be and what is. Although the two lovers lie "as if the cold flat of a blade / had winded us," he can hope for healing as he watches the water run down "the tilting stoups of your breasts" in a marvelous mixture of the liturgical and the erotic. Yet they cannot escape the "hot foreign night" that paralyzes them and makes the children cry, so that the only refuge from the hot dark night is the recollected image of the cool dark of a cave: "Yesterday rocks sang when we tapped / Stalactites in the cave's old, dripping dark— / Our love calls tiny as a tuning fork" (*WO,* 61). The love calls in the cave, like the love between them in the dark of the night and the dark of this moment in their marriage, is tiny but not lost. And if it is small, moreover, it is also, as suggested by the tuning fork, pure. That small human sound in the immense dark, that voice crying in the wilderness, while it promises nothing about the future, at least declares the future possible.

At the same time, the poem reiterates Heaney's interest in the old, subterranean dark, in the world hidden from normal view. That same interest expresses itself in these poems in sea imagery, particularly in "Shore Woman," "Maighdean Mara," and "Limbo." The last of these is about a baby found in the nets by salmon fishermen. Heaney imagines the mother's difficulty in drowning the child, "An illegitimate spawning," in the freezing water until her wrists were "dead as the gravel," then wading in with him "under / The sign of her cross." If the results are not as spectacularly different as the bog-drowned Tollund man, the experience nevertheless reminds the reader of the strangeness of the sea. This is an alien world where life is taken away and becomes the most alien of worlds in the last stanza:

> Now limbo will be
> A cold glitter of souls
> Through some far briny zone.
> Even Christ's palms, unhealed,
> Smart and cannot fish here.
>
> (*WO,* 70)

Heaven and hell we can understand; limbo has always appeared a bit out of focus, defined by what it is not rather than what it is. Heaney's sea imagery offers a brilliant analogy, with its "cold glitter of souls" like the salmon, denizens of a completely different element and therefore immune from our understanding. He recalls, moreover, the traditional fish imagery of Christianity, reminding us that even the Fisher of Souls would have no luck in these waters.

The foreignness of the sea is further reinforced in "Maighdean Mara," in some ways a companion piece to "Undine." In the earlier poem the water sprite wished for transformation into human form. In this poem the water being, in this case a mermaid, has spent eight years among humankind and is the worse for the experience. The theft of her magic garment, which seems to derive its power from the sea and thereby recalls Prospero's mantle in *The Tempest,* forces her to follow the thief and to share his bed, eventually bearing him children, in an attempt to reclaim the cloak and its powers. The man hides the garment in the eaves, and finally a thatcher weaves it into the roof; her hopes of ever recovering it evaporate. The mermaid undergoes her land experience with resentment and isolation: even her children remain distant from her. The hatefulness of the world of man drives her finally back to the sea, where, without her magic cloak, she presumably drowns. There is something more basic at stake here than simply the recounting of a folktale. The poem wants to push beyond its subject to examine the basic relationship between men and women: the man as predator, ravisher, destroyer; the woman as life-giver, certainly, but also resentful, trapped, smothered, yearning for escape. She does not fall into the easy tropes of traditional views of woman. While she may fulfill the roles of wife and mother, she does so by coercion, not choice. This theme appears in various guises in Heaney's work, sometimes on the personal level, sometimes, as in the poems of *North,* on a political or historical level.

That resentfulness also drives the voice of "Shore Woman." She, too, has had an experience of the otherness of the sea, as the mackerel fishing boat is surrounded (attacked, she believes) by porpoises. Her husband acts unconcerned by their antics, which terrify her and which she identifies as specifically male:

> the close irruption of that school,
> Tight viscous muscle, hooped from tail to snout,
> Each one revealed completely as it bowled out
> And over.
>
> (*WO,* 67)

Their aggressiveness, even if playful in this case, affronts her sensibility, although her husband scoffs at her fear, since it seems natural and normal to him. Her disgust with maleness also leads her to walk the shore at night, trapped between worlds hostile to her. In front of her lies the ocean and the threat of further encounters with the porpoises; behind her lies her husband, "Skittering his spit across the stove." It is a narrow strand of security, but security nevertheless, "I have rights on this fallow avenue, / A membrane between moonlight and my shadow." If the Shore Woman finds herself in an inhospitable world, she still labors to find and maintain a small piece she can look upon as her own. She exhibits the same stubborn refusal to yield, to be beaten, by superior force that characterizes the mermaid as well as other females in his poems, as well as his female Ireland, always fighting the unwanted advances or marauding raids of male England.

In the book's final poem Heaney discovers another foreign world, as he sits under a Rand McNally map of the moon, "The color of frogskin, / Its enlarged pores held / Open" (*WO,* 79). The moon becomes a vehicle of transporting him back in memory to his last evening in Donegal, "my shadow"

> Neat upon the whitewash
> From her bony shine,
> The cobbles of the yard
> Lit pale as eggs.
> (*WO,* 79)

The scene in Donegal is similarly unreal, objects transformed into something else, the light all bone and egg. He further recalls passing Good Friday services on his way out to fish by moonlight. His images of Ireland in this poem are singularly—one suspects willfully—peaceful; this landscape of traditional pieties and pleasures is as remote from the one in the newscasts as is the moon:

> Six thousand miles away,
> I imagine untroubled dust,
> A loosening gravity,
> Christ weighing by his hands.
> (*WO,* 80)

This final stanza is a marvel of double entendres. If the moon represents a "loosening gravity," that phrase can also stand for a goal, a dream, for

Heaney's native land, the possibility of a less grave situation in Northern Ireland. The "untroubled dust" of the moon, the antithesis of mankind, that troubled dust, also points to the Troubles in the North, which had reached a high pitch at the time *Wintering Out* was published. And the ultimate line offers not only Christ "weighing"—that is, balancing and judging—but "weighing" himself, hanging by his hands from the cross: the line gives us simultaneous images of judgment and redemption in a marvel of compression. Yet the dream is remote, imagined in a foreign place under an even more foreign sign. It may be that only there, removed from the site of the Troubles of Ulster, can Heaney entertain such a vision.

Strangeness is a key to much of *Wintering Out*—the past, the sea, the moon, the other sex, the underground. More than either of the earlier volumes, it explores the alien as a necessary component to understanding the familiar, the male to understanding the female, the past to understanding the present; nevertheless, it remains a transitional book, a bridge that makes a subsequent arrival possible. Heaney arrives at a full realization of the possibilities in *North,* one of the most powerful works in contemporary poetry.

Stations

During the same period when Heaney was publishing the poems of *Wintering Out* and *North,* he was working on a set of prose poems, first during his stay at Berkeley in 1970–71 and then again in Glanmore, County Wicklow, in 1973–74. On the whole, these poems follow a less ambitious program than either of the major volumes, sticking to what he describes in the brief preface as Wordsworthian "spots of time," telling incidents in his childhood and youth that help explain his own development. Many of the moments are of a completely personal nature: getting lost in the field behind the house, being kicked in the chest by a horse, making a muddy play-lake in the farmyard. Others involve relations, sometimes nervous, sometimes harrowing, between the Catholic and Protestant factions in Northern Ireland. What characterizes all the pieces of *Stations,* however, is a much more personal voice and sense of involvement than Heaney is wont to reveal in his conventional poems. While that immediacy sometimes makes for less than wholly successful art, it allows a better view of the poet in his social context.

Much of what Heaney reveals about himself will look familiar—in the sense of hostility, posed by nature, the agrarian way of life, the force exerted by religion—to readers of his earlier works. In "Waterbabies," for instance, he develops the small scene from childhood common to many early poems:

> We were busy in the fetid corner we christened Botany Bay. You pumped, I dammed. We opened sluice-gates, flooded mucky runnels and set sails by the black marina, penning white feathers into old potatoes. Sometimes a bomber warbled far beyond us, sometimes a train ran through the fields and small ripples quivered silently across our delta.
>
> Perversely I once fouled a gift there and sank my new kaleidoscope in the puddle. Its bright prisms that offered incomprehensible satisfactions were messed and silted: instead of a marvelous lightship, I salvaged a dirty hulk.[7]

The most immediately identifiable feature of this poem is its precise evocation of scene, so precise, in fact, that it calls attention to the worked-over quality of the reminiscence. All the hallmarks of a Heaney poem—the strong verbs, the exact diction, the surprising word choice (warbled), the extended metaphor—appear, lifting the rather unexceptional experience above the common run of such reminiscences. At their best, as here, these prose pieces rise to the level of the poet's verse, exerting the kind of force over us that we have come to expect. At the same time, however, it is impossible to see the advantage in the orthography of something like "Waterbabies," in which the rhythms as well as the imagery and language would lend themselves very conveniently to traditional verse form, particularly the free quatrains with which Heaney is experimenting at this point of his career.

One would seem to need more than mere novelty to recommend a form as exotic as the prose poem. Many of the poems are more loosely constructed than this one and are clearly not readily translatable into lined verse. Yet they also fail to work very convincingly as prose poems; they are often interesting but rarely compelling. None of these poems exhibits the kind of mastery of the form approaching that of, say, Geoffrey Hill in *Mercian Hymns* or Robert Bly in *The Morning Glory,* where the tension lies between the greater openness of the prose and the sudden sweep of language or imagery that provides an elevation.

Only rarely, as in "The Sabbath-breakers" or "Kernes," do the pieces really find their stride. In each case, the poem is a story. The first details a planned Sunday tournament of Gaelic football sabotaged by Protestants, ostensibly objecting to breaking the Sabbath. Here as elsewhere in the volume Heaney allows his own partisan feelings to show through his usual reserve, asking "what roundhead elders, what maypole hackers, what choristers of law and liberty" had perpetrated the vandalism. The match proceeds, of course, with the "tricolour," the Irish national flag, raised in the chestnut tree. "We lived there too," the poet declares. The scene he creates of players and spectators facing the tree for the anthem leaps forth as one of those sudden moments when he finds an appropriate emblem for the political circumstances faced in the North. "Kernes" is a word applied to both Scottish and Irish medieval foot-soldiers, and in this prose poem the descendants of the two meet each other. The Protestant boy, Dixon, accoutred with the very emblem of British conquest, a bicycle with the "rivetted breastplate of Sir Walter Raleigh," exchanges insults and slogans with Heaney and his Catholic friends. The piece's ability to show children acting out the forces of history, taking on their elders' fight as their own, gives it a despair for future peaceful settlement that has been present both in Heaney's subsequent work and in the course of Ulster's recent history. The poem achieves a kind of dynamism that the rest of the volume lacks, a liveliness and activity that suggests the choice of form is warranted.

What else the book offers is a look into the creative process, into the poet finding not so much his voice as his methods. While much of the book reworks earlier themes or stances running through the concurrent poetry, some of it also points ahead. "July" manages to do both, drawing phrases such as "a chosen people" from "The Other Side," while anticipating the reworking of this material in "Orange Drums, Tyrone, 1966" in *North.* The word "kernes" itself he will pick up in that volume's final poem as the escaped "wood-kerne." Perhaps most surprising is the image in "Cloistered" of the priest, with "his welted brogues unexpectedly secular under his soutane," a phrase that will be picked up almost verbatim nearly ten years later in "Station Island III." "Ballad" begins work on the memorializing poems that characterize much of both *Field Work* and *Station Island.* Indeed, these prose poems are themselves a kind of trial run, working out new forms, new attitudes, new stances that may appear in the later work, and for that reason, if for no other, they provide a valuable insight into the workings of the poet's craft.

Chapter Four
Merging Voice and Vision: *North*

Throughout his early career Heaney attends carefully to the composition of his books and the placement of poems within them. Not until *North,* however, does he construct a book as a unified, single piece of work. Much of the credit for that shift must go to his discovery of the possibilities offered by the bog people; while he clearly recognized the value of oddity and earth-memory, of ritual violence and appeasement of inscrutable forces in "The Tollund Man," noticing also the ways in which that discovery reinforced elements already present in his verse, *Wintering Out* lacks the driving, organizing force that the subsequent volume exhibits.

That force derives in large measure from the fascination these strange forms hold for him, as in "The Grauballe Man":

> The head lifts,
> the chin a visor
> raised above the vent
> of his slashed throat
>
> that has tanned and toughened.
> The cured wound
> opens inward to a dark
> elderberry place.
>
> (*N,* 35–36)

The corpse holds a mystery, as signified by the "dark elderberry place," a hint of hidden knowledge, of something internal that is masked by the spectacular outward appearance. Throughout the bog people poems, Heaney dwells on the marks of violence and victimage, calling one "my poor scapegoat," sensing the power their presence holds for him. He is not content, however, to let them go at that, as striking visual images; they imply too many connections with his own world and his own situation. They suggest to him, for one thing, the sort of intratribal violence he sees around him. Perhaps more importantly, though, they unlock the doors to the past; with their discovery "The soft-piled centuries / Fell open like a glib."

It would be a gross oversimplification to discuss *North* merely in terms of the bog poems, however, for while they occupy a major portion of the volume and inform much of the rest, they do not comprise its entirety. The first of the book's two sections consists largely of the ancient world, particularly the Viking north and Viking Ireland, suggested by the archaeological discoveries on the bogs of Jutland. Part 2 focuses on problems of contemporary Northern Ireland, although it remains enlightened by the historical perspective opened up by the first part. The past becomes more than a simple thematic construct in the book, as it so often is in the earlier poems. Rather, the appearance of the Grauballe man and his ilk open up the whole of the linguistic and poetic traditions; like Hamlet the "parablist" (whom he invokes in one poem), he holds up words for examination, digging back through etymologies to find their source. Similarly, he indulges his love of the Anglo-Saxon poetic in ways that lend a thematic unity to the poems. This discovery of the ways in which the past may be used to illuminate the present enables him, for the first time in his career, to write an entire volume with a single voice and single purpose, and the result is one of the major accomplishments of contemporary poetry.

The six bog poems—"Come to the Bower," "Bog Queen," "The Grauballe Man," "Punishment," "Strange Fruit," and "Kinship"—form the center, both thematically and physically, of *North,* as Heaney explores not only the significance of the archaeological finds themselves, but the whole range of possibilities those discoveries hold for his poetry. Part 1 of the book deals with the subject matter excavated from antiquity, some of it Hellenic, some of it Irish or Norse-Irish, and much of it Danish. The bog people poems act to unify the material from various ancient cultures; they are the link to the past:

Kinned by hieroglyphic
peat on a spreadfield
to the strangled victim,
the love-nest in the bracken,

I step through origins
like a dog turning
its memories of wilderness
on the kitchen mat.

(*N*, 40)

"Kinship" climaxes the bog poems and transports the poet most explicitly into the past, in order to compare it to the present. This long poem, consisting of six sections of six quatrains each, displays a remarkable movement from the commonplace to the marvelous to the political. In the first section, he presents readers with an old friend, Heaney the nature poet:

> I love this turf-face,
> its black incisions,
> the cooped secrets
> of process and ritual.
> (*N*, 40)

The blandness here seems a deliberate strategy, particularly in light of the poem's subsequent movement: the poet is establishing the reality of the bogs, their visual, auditory, and tactile qualities. The water "cheeps and lisps," the ground gives "spring" to his step, while the water is "not to be sounded / by the naked eye."

In the second section he begins playing with the sounds and derivations of words: "Quagmire, swampland, morass" (*N*, 41), all three traceable to Germanic roots, all with marvelous auditory traits, all (but especially "quagmire" and "morass") with moral or qualitative uses that extend metaphorically from the original, denotative meaning. He settles, however, on none of those but on the more neutral, less exotic *bog* in the second stanza. The bog is "ruminant ground," a marvelous double entendre, a place that swallows its cud ("mollusc / and seed-pod") only to yield it up again, not a place of reflection but a place that is itself reflective, thoughtful, a storehouse of memory or knowledge:

> Earth-pantry, bone-vault,
> sun-bank, enbalmer
> of votive gods
> and sabred fugitives.
>
> Insatiable bride.
> Sword-swallower,
> casket, midden,
> floe of history.

The lines are a dead stop, with their heavy caesurae and end-stops, the short lines and pounding rhythms. Because there are far more stressed than unstressed syllables, it is impossible to read these stanzas in any kind of familiar pattern; the poet has managed to overcome the natural—elsewhere, he claims tyrranical—pull of English versification toward iambic pentameter. Moreover, he employs the Old Norse, Anglo-Saxon *kenning,* the compound noun phrase, that is a major attribute of the book. Rarely, however, does he stack up as many of them in so short a space as he does in these two stanzas, even while mixing in Latinate phrasings: "votive," "fugitives," "Insatiable." The result of the kennings is to form double stresses that arrest the line's scansion, particularly in a line like "Earth-pantry, bone-vault," with its twin kennings and caesurae, its four stressed syllables out of five syllables total. The line is very much in the fashion of Anglo-Saxon verse, save for the absence of heavy alliteration. Elsewhere in the volume Heaney makes use of that device as well. The Anglo-Saxon line typically contained four stressed syllables, which for best effect should alliterate, and a mid-line break—the unstressed syllables did not figure into the count at all.

When he takes a different approach to the subject in section 3, though, describing his own digging in the bog, he abandons the tight, northern line in favor of a more open, conversational style. The act of digging takes on, as so often in his work, highly sexual overtones, with the male shovel entering the "insatiable bride" of the bog. Section 4 takes up the poetic self-consciousness in a more overt fashion, from the opening evocation of Yeats's "The Second Coming," "This centre holds" (*N,* 43), to the closing image of Heaney as a weeping willow tree reaching back always toward the earth. The bog-hole in this section is a "vowel of earth," and indeed the section is a compendium of vowel sounds, though still in the short-line quatrains whose length and stresses suggest free verse.

Still, the fascination the bogs hold for him is more than personal, more than merely poetic, and rests ultimately on the appearance of the stunning, leathery corpses of the bog people. Those ancient dead become one in the poem with the modern dead; the overt reasons are different, perhaps, but the sacrifice to some terrible deity, as in "The Tollund Man," remains the pattern for the act. So strong is the sense of kinship for Heaney that he invites Tacitus to return:

> Come back to this
> "island of the ocean"
> where nothing will suffice.
> Read the inhumed faces

> of casualty and victim;
> report us fairly,
> how we slaughter
> for the common good
>
> and shave the heads
> of the notorious,
> how the goddess swallows
> our love and terror.
>
> (*N*, 45)

These are no longer merely the victims of some lost ritual; rather, they are the emblems of a universal blood thirst, a need for taking life that manifests itself in only slightly different ways across millennia. Heaney senses the connection because he has watched the killings and has seen the faces of the dead, not only in Glob's work, where "seeing" requires an act of the imagination, but firsthand in his native country. In pushing back through time he finds corollary situations to his own: not only victimage and ritual, but occupying forces of a conquering foreign power as well. He also provides a response to Yeats's question in "Easter 1916," "O when may it suffice?" Heaney says that nothing—not the violence, not elections, certainly not the mere act of writing poems—will suffice. Through the irony of the last two stanzas Heaney connects the actions of contemporary Ulster with a universal blood thirst, a need for scapegoats and victims, and an obeisance to implacable, inscrutable forces represented by the "goddess," who is both Nerthus and Kathleen ni Houlihan (whom Heaney invokes in his discussion of the bog poems in *Preoccupations*) worshipped out of both "love and terror."

Always, though, Heaney focuses first of all on the appearance of the bog people, on their extreme otherness. If he tends to turn them into saints, he is brought up short by the wrinkled, leathery exterior, as in "Strange Fruit":

> Murdered, forgotten, nameless, terrible
> Beheaded girl, outstaring axe
> And beatification, outstaring
> What had begun to feel like reverence.
>
> (*N*, 39)

The figures simultaneously invite and repulse his worshipful impulses; while he may promise a pilgrimage to Aarhus, as he does in "The

Tollund Man," the association with the more immediate murders of Northern Ireland reminds him that these are, after all, victims of human frailty. "I almost love you," he declares to the adulterous girl in "Punishment," yet he also admits he would have cast "the stones of silence" (*N*, 38).

"Punishment" is a remarkable exercise in sympathetic imagination not only for its ability to place the poet in the position of the murdered girl, but for its ability to keep its distance even as it does so. In the opening stanzas, the poet claims to feel her sensory experience, the noose around her neck, the wind against her body. Even here, though, he puts distance between the two of them, as the wind "blows her nipples / to amber beads," already turning her from the living creature she was to a fossil, amber being composed of fossil resin. In stanza 3 he envisions her body anchored in the bog by a stone, yet in the following stanza that body becomes not human, but wood: "she was a barked sapling / that is dug up / oak-bone, brain-firkin." Her association with natural objects, a logical extension of her burial and preservation in the bog, tends to subvert the sympathy she commands as a human figure. Still, it does not undercut that fellow feeling so much that it makes her unrecognizable, for Heaney is also capable of pushing back beyond the inhuman aspects of her present form to see her as she was. If her shaved head now seems "a stubble of black corn," he also knows that she was once "flaxen-haired" and that "your / tar-black face was beautiful." He addresses her as "My poor scapegoat," yet also remains distant as the "artful voyeur."

The twin, opposed movements of his mind regarding her translates into an ambivalence, familiar by now, toward contemporary parallels:

> I who have stood dumb
> when your betrayed sisters,
> cauled in tar,
> wept by the railings,
>
> who would connive
> in civilized outrage
> yet understand the exact
> and tribal, intimate revenge.
> (*N*, 38)

If Heaney's position vis-à-vis the Troubles in Northern Ireland is difficult to pin down, this poem's ending has caused notable perplexities.

Ciaran Carson, one of the book's harshest critics, attacks what he sees as Heaney's excusing atrocities:

> It is as if he is saying, suffering like this is natural; these things have always happened; they happened then, they happen now, and that is sufficient ground for understanding and absolution. It is as if there never were and never will be any political consequences of such acts; they have been removed to the realm of sex, death, and inevitability.[1]

Conor Cruise O'Brien offers similarly negative analysis, that this poem, and the volume on balance, provides the bleakest view available of the state of Northern Ireland's affairs. Blake Morrison accuses Heaney of giving the killings in the North a "historical respectability" not provided by the daily press.[2]

It is worth noting that all three of these men are tied up with the Irish Question, that they seem to lack a perspective on the matter of violence in the poems. To return to the closing of "Punishment," the ambivalence grows out of Heaney's own unresolved feelings toward the strife. If the "civilized" man recognizes the wrongness of tar-and-feathering, of murder, of the various forms of violence, the poet's being is also broad enough and wise enough to acknowledge the impulse of the community to protect itself. There seems to me no attempt here to justify the atrocities, but only to "understand" (again, a distant sympathy), to comprehend their source. If Heaney belongs to the set of liberal-educated/English-speaking/reasonable adults, he also belongs to the set of native-Celt/Northern-Irish-Catholic nationalists. He may wish to speak with the voice of the first group; part of him, however, remains in touch with that second group, even its more extreme or unsavory parts. We may wish, with Carson, O'Brien, and Morrison, not to lend currency to the actions of the violent fringe, yet we must not deny the poet his *vision* (and Heaney has always insisted on the vatic function of poetry) and must therefore allow that artistic "seeing" is not the same thing as sanction. Moreover, the net result of the poet's recognition of the various elements is the characteristic paralysis; the ability to grasp simultaneously both poles of a diametric opposition translates into an inability to act, either to cast the stones or to stop those who do. In saving himself from the twin perils of a headlong plunge into the violence of the Provos on the one hand or easy condemnation on the other, the poet here becomes a victim of those historical forces he outlines so clearly.

One of the most striking aspects of all the bog poems, indeed of the poems generally in *North,* is the insistence on precise sensory detail. "The Grauballe Man" offers a catalog of specific descriptions and analogies, as it must, since Heaney declares that the man "lies / perfected in my memory" (*N,* 36): his heel is a "basalt egg," his "spine an eel arrested / under a glisten of mud," "his rusted hair / a mat unlikely /as a foetus's." The adjectives and nouns the poem offers in describing the Grauballe man almost uniformly derive from some wet environment, although not necessarily the bogs themselves. Indeed, the poem's weight comes almost entirely from the precision of the terms, as Heaney removes the man from the normal terminology of the dead, challenging us to call him "corpse" or "body," and elevates him instead to the rank of art.

Of course, that elevation might also apply to the act of writing itself, and as such this poem stands as one of the more self-reflexive of the bog poems. The Grauballe man is very much like the work that describes him: preserved, perfected, miraculous, eerie, memorable. As Neil Corcoran observes, the final stanza jars us out of the artistic revery with the forced recognition of the real, "with the actual weight / of each hooded victim / slashed and dumped."[3] Perhaps, though, Corcoran is too quick to release the poem and its subject from the realm of art. Certainly the closing image reminds the reader of the horror not only of the Grauballe man's death but also of those assassination victims of current social disruptions; on the other hand, throughout the poem, the operative metaphor has been a kind of birth, a coming into being, and even in the final lines the poem is still in the process of creation. Far from abandoning the artistic act, the writer is still making poetic hay off these victims of barbarity. It may be, as Corcoran suggests, that the "actual weight" of the dumped body acts "as a rebuke to Heaney's own mythologizing tendency," but if so, it does not stop him.[4] Heaney is fully capable, as he demonstrates elsewhere, of seeing the flaws in a position that, nevertheless, he declines to abandon. He will continue, moreover, to make art out of the very real victims of violence throughout his career.

Both "Bog Queen" and "Come to the Bower" also demonstrate the highly sensory approach as it slides into the overtly sensual. These two stand as companion pieces, the former from the point of view of the Bog Queen of Moira, the latter from the point of view of the discoverer of a body. The "queen" is particularly important for Heaney; since it stands as the first recorded discovery of a body in a bog in 1781 and comes not from Jutland but from south of Belfast, it provides a link between the Viking past (the woman is presumed to be a Viking) and Northern Ireland. Indeed, the poem could be construed as the cornerstone on which Heaney builds the book, allowing the connection between the two cultures to be more than metaphorical fancy.

"Come to the Bower," for its part, picks up and develops the digging metaphor so common in Heaney's work and operative in the preceding poem, "Bone Dreams," to offer a way into the bog poems (I have dealt with the sequence in very nearly reverse order). The more attractive metaphor of the piece, however, is of the woman's resting place in the bog as bower, which the poet pushes past its common meaning of arbor or leafy recess to its less customary use as boudoir. The focus of the action throughout remains on the physical activity of the archaeologist's hands removing the "dark-bowered queen" from her resting place: he must first "unpin" her, then "unwrap skins" to see her skull, and finally "reach" into the spot where she sleeps in a movement that is at once the simple act of freeing the body from the peat and a highly charged figurative sexual entry:

> I reach past
> The riverbed's washed
> Dream of gold to the bullion
> Of her Venus bone.
>
> (N, 31)

The poem equates the finding of the woman, and her sexuality, with treasure. The riverbed has only a "dream of gold," but her "Venus bone" becomes gold, while in the first stanza he has pushed beyond "the burst gizzards / Of coin-hoards" to find the body. Buried, rare, the woman is literally an equivalent to gold in archaeological value, but beyond that, she represents an alchemical miracle: an ordinary body transformed into a preserved, tanned body unlike its living form, an ordinary woman changed magically to not just the subject of a poem but an organizing metaphor for a volume of poems. The gold is for the poet as well as the researcher.

More typically, however, the golden quality stems from amber, rather than gold. The "Bog Queen," for instance, undergoes the process of becoming one with the earth, including "dreams of Baltic amber" (*N,* 33). That the amber is "Baltic" signifies the universality the poet invests in this lone Irish member of his bog pantheon. She is the unifying force of the volume, at once native Irish and connected to the Continent through her kinship with her Jutland cousins. Speaking for herself, she recounts the long, slow transformation she has undergone to become part of the landscape; in the bargain, she feels herself united with the whole of the earth. Like other earth dieties—Joyce's Finn MacCool, say—she becomes the defining point for the natural phenomena. The sun rises at her head, she tells us, and sets at her feet. At the same time, though, she explains her own preservation in terms of geology:

> My sash was a black glacier
> wrinkling, dyed weaves
> and pheonician stitchwork
> retted on my breasts'
>
> soft moraines.
> I knew winter cold
> like the nuzzle of fjords
> at my thighs—
>
> (N, 33)

Heaney presents an astonishing array of landscapes and cultures in two short stanzas. Throughout the poem, she speaks of a pervading sense of cold, for of course her roots are in the North countries; then, too, her period of burial resembles a winter's hibernation, just as her removal betokens the arrival of spring (the poet connects her with the fertility goddess to whom the bog men are sacrificed) or rebirth. In the above stanzas, the "nuzzle of fjords" becomes a critical phrase in connecting the woman to Viking culture and thereby in connecting the Irish past and the Viking past.

The bog poems, and "Bog Queen" more particularly, act as the pivotal point on which the volume turns. Most of part 1 to this juncture has concerned itself with Scandinavian history and instances of overlapping between that history and Ireland's. The remainder of book concerns itself primarily with Irish history, especially the backgrounds and events of the Troubles in Ulster. The bog poems attempt to legitimize the bond between the two movements as something more than the poet's caprice or novel coincidence; rather, in demonstrating a common blood culture, the sequence insists on the historical nature of society's violence against its members, not as a way of sanctioning that violence but of comprehending it.

Still, the more general association between the problems of Northern Ireland and the ancient northern warrior cultures and blood religions has already been established in the first part of the book. Each of the six poems preceding the bog sequence—"Belderg," "Funeral Rites," "North," "Viking Dublin: Trial Pieces," "The Digging Skeleton," and "Bone Dreams"—somehow links Ireland to the Viking past.

"Belderg" begins the process linguistically, playing with the root origins of "Mossbawn" and thereby drawing the Scandinavian past into the Irish present: "He crossed my old home's music / with older strains of Norse" (*N,* 14). Heaney plays his full bag of tricks with the name, identifying *bawn* as either a fort, a wall-mounded planter's house, or a corruption of the Irish *ban* for cotton, all maneuvers he rehearsed in a 1972 *Guardian* article. *Moss,* he tells readers there, is the Norse word for a bog, hence the crossing with "older strains" in the poem. The continuities extend into the physical realm as well, with the stone walls of an excavated Viking site in County Mayo mirroring exactly the patterns in contemporary Mayo. The archaeologist Tom Delaney converses with Heaney "about persistence, / A congruence of lives," as a way of explaining the remarkable similarities that endure across the space of a millennium. He demonstrates his own involvement with that persistence in the accumulation in his house of "growth rings / Of iron, flint, and bronze," signifying three ages of ancient mankind. In a sense, of course, we are all accumulations of the successive ages, unconscious inheritors of numerous traditions. Here, the poet, like the excavator, becomes aware of that heritage and in so doing awakens to the possibilities it suggests for understanding current as well as ancient history.

The poem employs three dominant metaphors for the continuity. The first, rather obviously, is the bog itself, the preserving force, the keeper of secrets. The initial focal point, the ancient quernstones from some Viking mill, were unearthed from the bogs, where, the poet surmises, they must have resembled eyes: "To lift the lid of the peat / And find this pupil dreaming / Of neolithic wheat!" To be able to strip away "the soft-piled centuries" as simply as lifting off the "blanket bog" gives the lie to the more customary understanding of the separation and lack of continuity between ages. One simply removes a bit of surface detail, the poem says, and the past is before one's eyes.

The stones themselves become the second metaphor; emblems of the past as well as vehicles for looking backward, they are both "a landscape fossilized" and "the eye of the quern" through which the poet passes, "Grist to an ancient mill," in the poem's final, surreal vision. The third image of endurance lies in the repeated references to trees, despite the absence of any real trees in the piece. The archaeologist refers to the growth rings in his home and later refers to the "Norse ring" on Heaney's tree as represented by the Norse root, *moss*. Heaney himself alludes to the "forked root" of the second syllable of his home farm. The stones and trees come together in a remarkable final image, as the quern's eye becomes the poet's mind's eye, where he sees "A world-tree of balanced stones, / Querns piled like vertebrae, / The marrow crushed to grounds." The world-tree, as Corcoran explains, "is the Yggdrasil of Norse mythology, the ash tree which sustained the Viking world in being."[5] That sustaining tree in *North* is less a tree of life than of death, persistence and congruity growing out of the eternal repetition of violence within the community. Many another bone turns up in the volume, and the importance of these figurative vertebrae in "Belderg" may lie in their implied violence: their sheer weight crushes the marrow, the life-supplying substance, out of existence. This closing image is a powerful omen of what the remainder of the book holds in store.

That omen remains implicit in the poem, the violence suggested rather than stated. In "Funeral Rites," on the other hand, the parallels between cultures and epochs becomes explicit, as Heaney muses on childhood deaths among family and friends, contemporary deaths from political violence, and the ancient Viking murders. The remembered funerals of Heaney's childhood form the basis of section 1 of the poem—ordinary, pedestrian, unremarkable: "dough-white hands," "the dulse-brown shroud," "eyelids glistening" (*N,* 16). Only when the boy Heaney encounters the corpses, the "Dear soapstone masks," whose "igloo brows" he kisses before the "black glacier" (a phrase he picks up again in "Bog Queen") of the funeral procession drives away, do the familiar dead become special, striking, and, most importantly, northern. The cortege becomes the focal point of the section 2, as the poet removes himself to a role of passive, powerless observer. The funeral glacier of memory, transformed into a serpent in the violent present, suggests the presence of evil in the current events, as does the oxymoron, "each neighborly murder." In the face of such evil, populace and poet alike are impotent to effect social change. "We pine for ceremony, / customary rhythms," he says, recalling, as Corcoran observes, Yeats's lines from "A Prayer for My Daughter," "How but in custom and ceremony / Are innocence and beauty born?"[6] The answer in Heaney's poem, as in "Easter 1916," must be that it is a terrible beauty, a beauty from which every shred of innocence has been stripped away. The funeral procession passes "each blinded home," intimating both the pulled blinds and the inhabitants blinded to events around them. The women left behind in "emptied kitchens" move through them "somnambulent," unhurried, to be sure, but volitionless, insensate, while "the whole country tunes / to the muffled drumming / of ten thousand engines." The drumming here brings to mind not only the literal sound of the automobiles but the drums of war and even—and for this reason the word choice may be infelicitous—the sectarian drumming of the Unionists commemorating the Battle of the Boyne each July.

In a brilliant sweep of imagery, the poem transports itself out of the present and into another past. Driving away from the wished-for sepulchres, it takes us past Strangford and Carlingford, changing them back, in a characteristic maneuver of linguistic archaeology, into "Strang and Carling fjords." Heaney deftly conjures up the Viking past of Ireland through the simple vehicle of place names, and suddenly we are taken out of the Troubles and back into Icelandic saga, where Gunnar's unavenged death broke the cycle of blood feuds and internecine retribution. The poet, however, can only envision the recent dead lying, like Gunnar, "joyful" in their tombs; only as an act of imagination can the current cycle of vengeance be broken. The Viking past in this poem becomes not only an analogous situation to the present, but one from which contemporary combatants could learn a valuable lesson. Significantly, it is the Viking culture, with its formal code of blood vengeance, not the Catholic or Protestant traditions of forgiveness and turning the other cheek, in which the cycle of violence is broken.

That transition in the third section of "Funeral Rites" also acts as a conduit into the Norse past for the poet, taking him into two poems directly concerned with that history. In "North" he imagines his way into the world of those "fabulous raiders," not as one of their descendants but as the descendant of their victims, again winnowing his way into the past by means of language. Throughout the poem Heaney relies primarily on words of northern—Anglo-Saxon and Norse—origin, words that carry him etymologically into that era he imagines. In the opening stanza he "returns" (the word suggesting a going back to the past) "to a *long strand,* / the *hammered shod* of a bay" (*N,* 19), the four italicized words all deriving from Germanic. Moreover, they play off one another, echoing consonantal and vowel patterns in a way which emphasizes the conscious choice to use them. Later, he refers to those Vikings "hacked and glinting / in the gravel of thawed streams" and to those lying beside "their long swords rusting," phrases in which every word stems from Old English or Norse, except "gravel," which comes from Old French. The poet avoids words of Greek or Latin origin so assiduously that when he employs one, as in the phrase "violence and epiphany," its appearance startles the reader into awareness of its basis and meaning. This strategy entails more than organic form, of which readers are rightly suspicious; rather, the heavy emphasis on words whose use in English predates the Norman invasion provides an imaginative point of entry into a history that otherwise remains remote and inaccessible. See here, the poem declares, the actions of these invaders have a bearing on our activity even now; we can scarcely talk or think without being touched by these early conquerors of the native Celts. All of English derives from the languages of conquering peoples: fewer than two dozen words survive into modern English from the Celtic languages spoken by the original inhabitants. In *North* generally, as in the title poem, Heaney strains against the commonness of the language to make it strange to us, to regain its foreign qualities, to emphasize its imposition from without upon the residents of Ireland.

The second point of entry into the Viking period is the sea itself. The poet, standing by the "Atlantic thundering," finds himself unmoved by "the unmagical / invitations of Iceland, / the pathetic colonies / of Greenland," while the Viking raiders speak to him in "ocean-deafened voices" "lifted again / in violence and epiphany." More specifically, the entire Viking culture speaks to the poet, not through the vaguely disembodied remains of the warriors themselves but, in a brilliant and bold metaphor, through the "longship's swimming tongue." The predatory Viking ship, with its elongated prow, metamorphoses into a giant snake, probing, also predatory, with all the attendant connotations of consciencelessness and eroticism—it is well to remember the poet's insistence on Ireland as the female victim of masculine raiders in this context—which our culture attaches to that image. To this voice he attributes a wonderful clarity of hindsight, although prescience might be more accurate, since its description of its own culture applies so perfectly to the poet's as well:

> the hatreds and behindbacks
> of the althing, lies and women,

exhaustions nominated peace,
memory incubating the spilled blood.
(*N*, 20)

"Althing" is a wonderful word in this context; both an archaism for everything and the word for the Icelandic Parliament, it suggests the whole of a culture and at the same time its specifically political realm. In these poems, the bogs of Jutland notwithstanding, Heaney looks more typically to Iceland, lying as it does only a few degrees west of due north from Ireland, rather than to Norway or Denmark for the Viking heritage.

Given the uneasy contemporary social situation, the longship-serpent counsels the poet to throw himself into his poetry:

It said, "Lie down
in the word-hoard, burrow
the coil and gleam
of your furrowed brain.

Compose in darkness.
Expect aurora borealis
in the long foray
but no cascade of light.

Keep your eye clear
as the bleb of the icicle,
trust the feel of what nubbed treasure
your hands have known."

This is, of course, the advice Heaney has already been following in the book: he has elected to lie in the word-hoard, sifting through the treasures he finds there, plucking out this specimen, discarding that, always turning inward, examining how the external conditions express themselves or are explained by his own thought processes. *North* is very much a book composed in darkness, bleak and subterranean, with flashes of light, some of which, as in the book's final lines, elude the poet.

This poem stands as the first of a lengthy series in which a voice offers Heaney wisdom very much in line with the direction his poetry would in any event take; they recur throughout the subsequent books, most notably in several poems in the "Station Island" sequence. Certainly, convenience recommends the advice to "trust the feel of what nubbed treasure" in a volume built around the central metaphor of that other nubbed treasure, the bog people. Still, if the tone is perhaps self-congratulatory, there is also an air of defensiveness, a preemptory strike against those who, like Ciaran Carson, accuse this book of failing to engage the political realities, to take a firm stance regarding the violence. The poet's only rightful provenance, he tells us through the longship's voice, is his poetry. Indeed, his career demonstrates a wary relationship to current events: Politics remains a proper subject only as long as it can be subsumed in personal or historical or mythological contexts. The moment it threatens to overcome the poetry and draw him into pronouncement or *engagement,* Heaney withdraws.

Many of the images of "North" recur in "Viking Dublin: Trial Pieces," whose ostensible starting point is a design drawn on a piece of bone, a part of the *Viking Dublin* exhibition at the Irish National Museum. In the poem's six sections, each comprised of four short-line, free quatrains, Heaney brings to bear an amazing sum of information, erudition, and insight. In the marvelous ambiguity of the opening line of section 2, "These are trial pieces, / the craft's mystery," he further insists on developing the parallel between subject and poem. On magnified inspection, what appeared at first to be "a swimming nostril" becomes "a migrant prow / sniffing the Liffey," the serpentine figure from the previous poem.

Throughout the first three stanzas the poem turns inward on itself, employing metaphors drawn from its own creation. The repeated references to handwriting, to calligraphy, all focus attention on the act of writing, upon "the craft's mystery" as he calls it: The eel lost in the basket of eel, the line of calligraphy that "amazes itself," the ship "swanning it up to the ford," and even the description of the ship lodging in the bank, its "hull / spined and plosive / as *Dublin.*" This last figure points to a definite strategy of the poem, the intermingling of objective and verbal levels of meaning, of language and referent. If the poem seems to follow the conceit offered by its subject, that conceit is developed in terms of the act of writing the poem, so that the question of primacy—Does the subject lead to the poem or does the poem create its subject?—becomes impossible to unravel. In this playful handling of self-referentiality, Heaney shows himself to be very much a postmodernist writer.

Yet just when the poem appears most in danger of disappearing into its own device, it bursts out, pointing away from itself. At the beginning of the fourth stanza, the design of the longship has entered "my longhand," itself "cursive," describing the tortuous path of a worm through the mud, when suddenly the conceit gives way to another:

> I am Hamlet the Dane,
> skull-handler, parablist,
> smeller of rot
>
> in the state, infused
> with its poisons,
> pinioned by ghosts
> and affections,
>
> murders and pieties,
> coming to consciousness
> by jumping in graves,,
> dithering, blathering.
> (*N*, 23)

Like the prince, the poet engages death and mystery, as expressed in the marvelous line mixing Old English–style kenning, "skull-handler," and the Latinate "parablist." And while he may point out the troubles in the state, he is also, like Hamlet, corrupted by them, caught up in all the prejudice and loyalties, the "murders and pieties." Then too, of course, Heaney has taken to "jumping into graves" as a means of "coming to consciousness," if we understand that phrase to mean the awakening of his art to the possibilities adumbrated by the bog people.

When in stanza 5, then, he describes the Vikings, readers can immediately see the explicit parallel with contemporary Ulster society:

> neighbourly, scoretaking
> killers, haggers
> and hagglers, gombeen-men
> hoarders of grudges and gain.
> (*N*, 24)

The passage recalls both the "neighbourly murder" of "Funeral Rites" and Heaney's recounting of the wall in Belfast after Bloody Sunday when, on 30 January 1972, thirteen civilians, all Catholics, were killed by members of the Royal Ulster Constabulary: "PARAS THIRTEEN, the walls said, / BOGSIDE NIL."[7] Significantly, the stanza form itself, even more so here than in the rest of the poem, insistently transports readers into that earlier era. With its hard consonants, short lines, and repeated caesurae, the stanza rebuffs any attempt to read it in terms of iambic feet or standard meter. Instead, it scans as Old English scanned, by virtue of its alliteration and its heavy stresses rather than any set number of syllables in the line. Throughout the volume, the short, variable-foot lines oppose our expectations, fighting against what Geoffrey Hill has called "the inertial drag of the language." By moving so deliberately against the history of English verse, by folding modern English, which fits so comfortably into iambic rhythms, back against an archaic prosody, *North* astonishes its audience into a new awareness of the history of the language and a new way of hearing or reading poetry. This poem's sense of its place in language owes something to Joyce, whose *A Portrait of the Artist as a Young Man* it invokes, "Old fathers, be with us," in claiming descendancy from the Vikings.

The poem's final section leads back to the National Museum, by way of Jimmy Farrell in J. M. Synge's *Playboy of the Western World,* who speaks of the skulls there, which give way, in a truly startling image, to "the skull-capped ground" of "the cobbled quays" of Dublin.

This sense of overwhelming, uncontained death carries over into the following poem, "The Digging Skeleton," which Heaney identifies as "After Baudelaire" rather than a translation from Baudelaire, a wise distinction since, although the poem retains the *a b b a* rhyme scheme and the general outline of the poem, the new version is pure Heaney. For instance, he translates the line "Bechant comme des laboureurs" as "Digging the earth like navvies" (*N,* 25): the rendering, while literally accurate, is typical of his own work and predisposition. Some of his changes are wonderful, if free-form, as when he gives us the line "Epouvantable et clair embleme" as "Death's lifers," a phrase to be preferred as both more concise and more vivid. The poem displays Heaney's gift for line construction, as he departs from the French original's regular metrics in favor of Patrick Kavanagh's free quatrains, which vary considerably in line length from one to another. Moreover, there is genius behind the line and stanza breaks that delay crucial information: " 'This is the reward of faith / / In rest eternal. Even death / lies.' " In each case, the intervening space allows readers to pause on the noun so that the subsequent word or phrase surprises. Both instances further the poem's development of a sense of the unquiet dead, a sense that perhaps presages the poet's interest in Dante in his subsequent poetry. For now, Baudelaire's piece allows Heaney to examine the dead he has been holding up for study, and to question his own motives, as they tell him that "Some traitor breath" refuses their desire for simple rest, " 'our one repose / When the bleeding instep finds its spade.' " The work of art—the anatomical plate, the Baudelaire poem, the Heaney bog people poem—robs the grave, steals peace from the corpses, puts them to work.

The concerns and attitudes of these poems come together in "Bone Dreams," which serves both as a culmination of the specifically Irish archaeological poems and a leaping off point for the bog poems to follow. As with "Viking Dublin: Trial Pieces," Heaney finds his way into the poem by means of a piece of bone, this one unadorned by design: the bone as object rather than artifact. Again, the physical and linguistic levels interact as he studies in this "rough, porous / language of touch." The direction of the poem is entirely backward, toward the past that causes the poet to write in a language other than Gaelic. To that end, he uses the bone figuratively as well as literally to convey him in imagination to a source, whipping the fragment in

> the sling of mind
> to pitch it at England
> and follow its drop
> to strange fields.
> (*N*, 27)

The stanza may on one level cast Heaney as a poetic David, also a poet, casting his stone at the English Goliath; certainly a sling is a weapon, and there have been those among the ultra-conservative faction in Ulster's Protestant community who see Heaney's work in that light, as enemy propaganda. Yet the projectile lands harmlessly among the foreign and exotic.

The most fascinating element of those strange fields lies on the linguistic, poetic level, as the kenning "Bone-house," variously defined in the *Oxford English Dictionary* as "charnel house, coffin, or body," which he later takes back to "*ban-hus,*" becomes not just a word but an object, like the bone itself, to be held up for study. Heaney has told Neil Corcoran that his interest in Viking archaeology was fueled by the excavations and rethinking about that culture going on in Dublin when he moved there in the early seventies and by his association with the archaeologist Tom Delaney, memorialized in "Station Island VII," although he himself studied the field "not very systematically."[8] His study, however, has been much more thorough in the archaeology of poetics and language, and in section two he leads readers back to the source:

> I push back
> through dictions,
> Elizabethan canopies,
> Norman devices,
>
> the erotic mayflowers
> of Provence
> and the ivied latins
> of churchmen
>
> to the scop's
> twang, the iron
> flash of consonants
> cleaving the line.
> (*N,* 28)

Each of the stages of literature or language he mentions in the passage has been visited upon Ireland from outside; a study of literary form involves a study of invading forces, as the changes have come about largely as a result of changes introduced by new conquerors either of Ireland or of England herself. The passage holds serious political implications as well: what he uncovers in this poem as in the whole volume is the knowledge that both sides of the civil strife are fighting someone else's fight, that all elements in the struggle are imported. Not only are the British, and by extension Ulster Protestantism (which has been in the country for "only" three centuries), alien, but so is the Catholicism to which the northern minority so staunchly adheres. Neither religious affiliation is native to the island. The language in which Heaney works, as well as most of the literary heritage that informs his writing, is also foreign. Even back at its earliest level, represented here by "the scop's twang," the English poetic tradition remains distant, other, simultaneously familiar and alien.

These warring forces create in Heaney's work what Merle Brown identifies in contemporary English verse generally as a "double lyric," twin opposed impulses, such as those toward community and divisiveness, that generate an inner argument, the unresolved poles of a dialectic whose synthesis is not a third position but simultaneous utterance issuing from each center. In *North* those forces express themselves most commonly in terms of two communities, the factional Catholic and the broader Northern Irish, or of writing in a language that ceaselessly reminds the writer of the ways it excludes or oppresses him. The poet responds by trying to push back beyond factionalism, beyond the language question, "past / philology and kennings," to reach a point at the far reaches of memory. There, in sections 4 and 5, the poem creates an astonishing mix of landscape, literature, and eroticism that articulates the full extent of the poet's ambivalence toward England. Having plunged "beyond" the tradition, he arrives at a sort of pastoral love poem whose object is both British topography (Hadrian's Wall, the neolithic Maiden Castle southwest of Dorchester, the earthworks Giant carved on the chalk-downs of Cerne Abbas) and the language itself, the pure sound of English speech: "the vallum of her brow / and the long wicket / of collar-bone." The variety of the vowels even in this short passage reminds the reader again of Heaney's ability to manipulate the language, to transform words into music. Although he may be trapped by circumstance into writing in English, he scarcely seems, for all that, a victim. In a gigantic inflation worthy of *Finnegans Wake,* he depicts himself as more than the match for England. When in the sixth section of the poem, then, he finds a dead mole in Devon—an animal not found, significantly, in Ireland—his identification with it, "small and cold / as the thick of a chisel," it too a digger, illuminates the opposition present in his feelings about himself as well as his subject. Simultaneously a stone giant and a tiny burrower, he encounters a literature attractive in its possibilities and repugnant in its historical associations.

The same dynamics exert themselves in "Act of Union," except that this poem gives voice to the possessor. The Act of Union of 1800 created the United Kingdom of Great Britain and Ireland, although Heaney exploits the clearly sexual overtone, turning the parliamentary act into a political mating. England in the poem is the "tall kingdom over your shoulder," solicitous perhaps, but nevertheless "still imperially / male." The coupling has brought pain to the woman in the form of childbirth, which in turn "sprouted an obstinate fifth column / Whose stance is growing unilateral." The immediate association of the reader will very likely be that the issue of this pairing are the Unionists, for whom Heaney clearly feels little sympathy. The image of his heart as a "wardrum" may further such a reading. Yet the "parasitical / and ignorant little fists" that threaten both mother and father seem less those of faction than of civil violence more generally. The Act of Union, following in the tradition of English imperialism in Ireland, virtually guaranteed a future of insurrection and internecine violence that ended in the South only with independence and that, in the six counties, continues unabated to this day.

"Act of Union," one of the least convincing of the poems in part 1, fails largely because the voice itself seems forced, seems to mouth the words the poet chooses for it rather than to find its own words. Throughout his career, looking back to a poem like "Docker" in his first book, Heaney has had difficulty representing the other side. Perhaps he is too much entangled—perhaps everyone in Ulster is—with one side to be able to see the other clearly. He attempts to balance his view of the Troubles in his poetry, seeing both sides as victims of a situation not of their making, yet as he has told Seamus Deane, he is inevitably situated in a narrow political and religious moment:

> Poetry is born out or the watermarks and colourings of the self. But that self is some ways takes its spiritual pulse from the spiritual structure of the community to which it belongs; and the community to which I belong is Catholic and nationalist. . . . I think that poetry and politics are, in different ways, an articulation, an ordering, a giving of form to inchoate pieties, prejudices, world-views, or whatever. And I think that my own poetry is a kind of slow, obstinate, papish burn, emanating from the ground I was brought up on.[9]

That "slow burn" may make it impossible for the poet to give full sympathy to the other community is such a divisive situation; there are certainly pressures from within his own, as he demonstrates in the "Station Island" sequence, not to. And the result, the dual impulses toward loyalty and understanding, toward the smaller community and the larger, create a double voice, the tension, that so often informs his verse. The "slow burn" will also be located much more clearly in his own historical moment in part 2, but before moving on, we must look at the two Antaeus poems with which he frames part 1.

In these poems, Antaeus is made to serve more than one function, both the native, earth-loving force representing Ireland against Hercules' greater power and cunning that is England and "the pieties of illiterate fidelity" against Hercules' "balanced rational light," as he expresses it to Deane.[10] The poet allows himself the anachronism of Greek myth in these poems because Antaeus' reliance on the earth as the source of strength fits so well thematically in the context of the book. The Irish, too, have been lifted from their land and so destroyed.

In the first poem, "Antaeus" (dated 1966), the giant lives secure inside the earth in his cave, "cradled in the dark that wombed me" (*N,* 12), secure in the knowledge of his strength. As Marx observed, however, every movement carries with it the seeds of its own destruction, and even here, he can foresee the possibility of his destruction, that some hero, "sky-born and royal," may plot the giant's "elevation, my fall." The companion poem then begins with the very words, "Sky-born and royal," and the reader knows even without benefit of the legend that Antaeus is doomed. In crushing Antaeus, Hercules elevates him into a mythic level of a different sort, "high as a profiled ridge, / a sleeping giant," one of those earth figures, like the one at Cerne Abbas or like Finn MacCool, who become the repositories of local superstition or the symbols of community hopes, the "pap for the dispossessed." The remarkable aspect of the poem is that its origin, as Heaney explained to John Haffenden, grew out of a conversation about poetry with Iain Crichton Smith:

> He's got a kind of Presbyterian *light* about him. The image that came into my mind after the conversation was of me being a dark soil and him being a kind of bright-pronged fork that was digging it up and going through it. . . . That kind of thinking led into the poetry of the second half of *North,* which was an attempt at some kind of declarative voice.[11]

The poetic and political levels become largely indistinguishable in this analysis, as Heaney identifies himself, as he does in *North,* as both the dark soil and Gaelic in ancestry, Catholic in religious background, nationalist in political affiliation. In part 2 he deals specifically with his location within that matrix, recognized throughout part 1 but always held in a larger historical or mythopoeic context.

Northern Ireland's occupation by Britain is only the most recent in a long series of occupations by foreign nations, and the British soldiers in modern Derry and Belfast represent a link to the Roman legions and Viking raiders. Political and nationalistic violence had become, by the time Heaney had written *North,* commonplace, and their pull on the poet, on any writer, was powerful. But Heaney the artist—whatever Heaney the citizen may think of circumstance in Ulster—recognizes that surface appearances can be misleading, and so he pushes through surfaces, cuts into the earth to excavate the historical basis for the Troubles, examines his demotic tongue and his literary traditions to ferret out the sources of oppression and strife. Surfaces belong, as he points out in a 1971 *Listener* essay, to another medium:

I am fatigued by the continuous adjudication between agony and injustice, swung at one moment by the long tail of race and resentment, at another by the more acceptable feelings of pity and terror. We live in the sickly light of TV screens, with a pane of selfishness between ourselves and the suffering. (*P,* 30)

From the television and newspaper journalists and from politicians, Heaney suggests in "Whatever You Say Say Nothing": "Who proved upon their pulses 'escalate,' / 'Backlash' and 'crack-down,' 'the provisional wing,' / 'Polarization' and 'long-standing hate' " (*N,* 57). The people of Ulster learn to transform the terrible realties of bomb explosions and internment camps into hollowly pious Orwellian terminology and to survive in a place "where to be saved you must only save face / And whatever you say, you say nothing" (*N,* 59). The poem ostensibly grows out of an encounter with an English journalist collecting opinions on "the Irish thing," and the resulting lines are a compendium of the hollow phrases and stock responses that characterize the behavior of residents and observers of the six counties. Against those cheap homilies, the poem counterposes the violent reality. Section 1 ends with a litany of the standard statements, all of them empty, easy:

"Oh, it's disgraceful, surely, I agree,"
"Where's it going to end?" "It's getting worse."
"They're murderers." "Internment, understandably . . ."
The "voice of sanity" is getting hoarse.

Against the safety of the responses that run throughout the first section, the second opens with a very matter-of-fact account of circumstances: "Men die at hand. In blasted street and home / The gelignite's a common sound effect."

Through it all, Heaney hears the voice of a giant over his shoulder, speaking out of other Irish Troubles. When in "Whatever You Say Say Nothing" he ends a line with "bangs," he acknowledges the presence: "It's tempting here to rhyme on 'labour pangs' / and diagnose a rebirth in our plight / / But that would be to ignore other symptoms" (*N,* 58). Heaney foresees no birth of a terrible beauty. Yet he senses the kinship with Yeats, the wrestling with a national crisis of terror and violence, the urge to put current problems into historical perspective, the search for a coherent private mythology at once aesthetically satisfying and capable of making the world comprehensible, the minority status (although Yeats's minority was the other one, and in the South, and privileged), the constant struggle to avoid the Scylla of propaganda on the one hand and the Charybdis of escapism on the other. And so his digging leads him not to the distant past only, but also to a recent ancestor.

Invoking Yeats in the second section puts the events described therein into perspective: against the journalistic cliché, the very real violence of the Troubles threatens to pull the country apart, in much the same way the Easter Rebellion and its aftermath did in the South earlier in the century. Like Yeats, Heaney takes an uneasy midpoint position on the strife, unwilling totally to condemn or valorize either side. Also like Yeats, he is unable to repress his instinct to take sides. As a result, the section threatens to pull itself apart. At the end of it he bemoans his inability to create a satisfactory poem, "To lure the tribal shoals to epigram / And order." While he tries to present a balanced view, using Conor Cruise O'Brien's phrase in noting that "On all sides the 'little platoons' are mustering," his own memory of involvement drags him into the fray. He identifies himself as one of the minority accustomed to "Long sucking the hind tit" that "leaves us fork-tongued on the border bit," and further on he makes a highly partisan comparison with the explosions and gunfire that have become common: "Last night you didn't need a stethoscope / To hear the eructation of Orange drums / Allergic equally to Pearse and Pope." Clearly, the side that opposes nationalism and Catholicism is the *other* side, and for all his liberal-mindedness (and this he acknowledges) Heaney cannot overcome the alterity of the Unionists to embrace them fully as fellows in the struggle for peace.

The poem's strategy, then, is to accept and announce its own biases and to work through them, not to arrive at solution or even understanding, but to comprehend its (and its creator's) limitations. In section 3 he examines the effects of "The famous / / Northern reticence, the tight gag of place / and times," reciting a litany begun at the end of section 1 of safe, nonpartisan phrases. In response, he wishes to tear down the walls, which he identifies as "dykes the Dutchman built," between classes and religious groups, "Yet for all this art and sedentary trade / I am incapable." If, as he is told in one early poem, the pen is truly lighter than the spade, it has its failings as an instrument for either constructing or dismantling. In a place where names, schools, addresses, manners of speaking all identify one's place in a society divided almost to the brink of civil war, mere versifying, for Heaney as for Yeats before him, cannot hope to satisfy the desire for resolution.

What he offers instead is something of a found poem, the one previously used as the dedication to *Wintering Out*. Section 4 offers yet another view of the poet simultaneously touched and cut off from his surroundings; safely within his automobile, he views the internment camp of Long Kesh (now Maze Prison), at first as something almost from outer space, with the bomb crater in the roadside, the machine gun posts, and the ground fog, but then as something much more familiar, if no more comforting, "some film made / Of Stalag 17, a bad dream with no sound" (*N*, 60). This scene, however alien, seems not quite real; surely, the poet seems to say, things cannot have got quite so far as this. In an attempt to understand, he retreats to more familiar scenes:

> Is there a life before death? That's chalked up
> In Ballymurphy. Competence with pain,
> Coherent miseries, a bite and sup,
> We hug our little destinies.

The poem's retreat mirrors that of the residents: in the face of the extraordinary, the horrific, there is comfort to be drawn from the quotidian exigencies, the small life. Throughout his work, Heaney finds himself pulling away from direct engagement with the social upheaval in his native land. That strategy is necessary in order to gain the perspective required to examine the historical and linguistic forces behind the unrest, yet that distance can also be a liability, removing the poet too far from the immediacy of the Troubles that informs and vivifies his work.

Throughout the second part of the book, the underlying tensions in the language speak through the more relaxed syntax to constantly remind the reader of the historic origins of the violence and of contemporary discrimination based on dialect. In "The Ministry of Fear" he writes of dialect as a litmus test of caste and of writing a poem in which he

> innovated a South Derry rhyme
> With *hushed* and *lulled* full chimes for *pushed* and *pulled.*
> Those hobnailed boots from beyond the mountain
> Were walking, by God, all over the fine
> Lawns of elocution.

Words, ways of phrasing, accents, names all help identify a speaker in Ulster. One has only to listen in order to recognize a potential ally or adversary, and the citizenry is always listening for those clues, "Besieged within the siege, whispering morse," as he says in "Whatever You Say Say Nothing." The atmosphere of mistrust, suspicion, and fear arises from differences in language, and those differences in turn arise from history: who conquered Ireland when, and what did they leave behind? Dialectical differences reinforce the class system and prejudice and are a result of a history of conquest, of what the poet calls "the ground possessed and repossessed."

"Singing School," the closing sequence of six poems, explores dialect as one part of a multiplicity of forces conspiring against the citizen, particularly the Catholic citizen, of Ulster. "The Ministry of Fear," which he dedicates to fellow poet and scholar Seamus Deane, looks at education, largely a segregated undertaking, and the terrors involved in growing up, ranging from condescending statements about the Catholics' use of English to policemen stopping the young Heaney as he returns from a date. In the following poem, "A Constable Calls," the mundane and the threatening are brought together, as the policeman who comes to take the farm census for tax purposes transforms metonymically into his accoutrements: his revolver, police boots, riot baton, and heavy ledger (itself a sort of economic weapon, which Heaney calls, unsurprisingly, a "domesday book"). The constable pedals off at the end without incident, although Heaney's father has not confessed the row of turnips in the back of the potato field. Nevertheless, the presence of the emblems of official violence establishes a credible threat to the young Heaney, wrapped up as he is in "Arithmetic and fear." The official quality of fear further displays itself in "Orange Drums, Tryone, 1966," in which Heaney describes the activity of a single drummer in a July celebration commemorating the victory of William of Orange over James II at the Battle of the Boyne in 1690, which victory led to the establishment of the Anglo-Scots Protestant population in Ireland. The language of the poem is violent: the drums, "lodging thunder / Grossly," take over the celebration as they take over the drummers; they "preside, like giant tumours," over the celebration; "The pigskin's scourged until his knuckles bleed." This drum is a weapon as well as an instrument, its power sound, its message antipapist. Heaney, as a Catholic, clearly feels its threat in the air, "pounding like a stethoscope." The forces of government, which are in British hands, in Northern Ireland seem arrayed against the Catholic minority, against those who seek home rule or self-determination.

Heaney finds the appropriate emblems for this repressive atmosphere, however, not in Belfast but in Madrid. In the fourth poem of the sequence, "Summer 1969," he burrows into the very nature of society's violence against its own citizens. On holiday in Spain when the current round of civil unrest began in 1969, the poet experienced the outbreak at great distance, "suffering / Only the bullying sun of Madrid." Yet throughout the poem Spain and Ireland are inextricably linked. The smell of the fish-market rises "like the reek off a flax-dam," recalling the title poem from *Death of a Naturalist;* later, the "patent leather of the Guardia Civil / Gleamed like fish-bellies in flax-poisoned waters" (69). Almost immediately afterward, the poem invokes "Lorca from his hill" where he was killed by the Guardia Civil. The television brings both "death counts and bullfight reports" to the expatriate, mingling Spanish and Irish forms of violence. These two forms come together in the poem's final movement, when the "Constabulary cover[ing] the mob / Firing into the Falls" of the opening is echoed in the poet's viewing of Goya's "Shootings of the Third of May" in the Prado, where that painting of official violence "Covered a wall." The echo of *covered* simply emphasizes a parallel already abundantly clear. As he looks at this and other Goya pieces—violent, startling, powerful—he feels a sort of kinship with the painter in terms of placement within history, although their positions relative to that history differ widely: "He painted with his fists and elbows, flourished / The stained cape of his heart as history charged." One might be tempted to object, with Edna Longley, at the bravado and local color of the poem's closing,[12] yet the lines turn against their maker, whose encounter with history is much like his encounter with bullfighting, limited to viewing it on television. Neither Lorca nor Goya can be the model for a poet who feels himself, unavoidably, too withdrawn from events of the moment. Rather, his model must lie closer to home, in the form of a poet who watched earlier Irish unrest through the window of his tower and interpreted it through the grid of his own private mythology. Like Yeats, he finds himself trapped by language and self-enforced distance from events, "an internal emigré, grown long-haired / And thoughtful." The neutrality and the excavation are not without their dangers; in the final poem Heaney acknowledges his cost for staring too long at the ground, fixing on the metaphor of a wood-kerne, a foot soldier from earlier uprisings who took to the woods to avoid the bloodshed:

Escaped from the massacre,
Taking protective colouring
From bole and bark, feeling
Every wind that blows;

Who, blowing up these sparks
For their meagre heat, have missed
The once-in-a-lifetime portent
The comet's pulsing rose.
(*N*, 73)

Heaney appears to understand both the advantages and the costs of his distancing himself from the violence in Ulster. Of course he can never be free of the circumstances in the six counties; of course the events there inform his writing; of course he is constantly touched on imaginative and personal levels. Still, the lens through which he views those events, while bringing some elements into focus, blocks others from view. Throughout "Singing School" he wrestles with the problems of involvement and withdrawal, arriving at an acceptance of what is probably an inevitable, if not altogether satisfactory, situation. An earth-grubber like Antaeus (the "pulsing rose" echoes the book's opening poem), Heaney finds himself cut off from the light that may be royal and sky-born. At the same time, the poem, like the book as a whole, argues against him. He is fully able to describe the comet, "Those million tons of light / Like a glimmer of haw and rosehips." The final ground of poetry is within the poet rather than outside, whatever Heaney's misgivings that he has not done enough, and the poem, like the book it closes, marvelously realizes its inner mission. This may be the real achievement of *North,* that it is able, despite the poet's fears of isolation, to engage its historical and political setting imaginatively and symbolically and thereby arrive at a level of truth it might not reach through a more direct treatment of the Troubles: a Yeatsian strength of voice and vision in the face of personal ambivalence.

Chapter Five

Loosening the Forms: *Field Work*

In his next volume Heaney expands his propensity to dig and finds a new function: burier and elegist. At once a much more private and much more public book than its predecessor, *Field Work* concerns itself not with the distant corpses of Jutland or the comparative abstractions of victims of "national strife," but with the poet's own dead relatives and friends. Some are casualties of the sectarian violence—the friend whose "candid forehead stopped / A pointblank teatime bullet," the cousin flagged down in the road and killed, the old fisherman "blown to bits / Out drinking in a curfew." This last victim, in "Casualty," recalls Yeats's fisherman for whom the poet wishes to write a poem "as cold and passionate as the dawn." Like Yeats's character, Heaney's is a model of isolation and self-sufficiency; he requires not society but his own:

> But he would not be held
> At home by his own crowd
> Whatever threats were phoned,
> Whatever black flags waved.
> (*FW*, 22)

Unlike Yeats's fisherman, however, this one cannot simply go his own way, for despite his solitude he is drawn into the pattern of random violence, murder by lot. Yet it is that fatal independence that Heaney finds so attractive:

> To get out early, haul
> Steadily off the bottom,
> Dispraise the catch, and smile
> As you find a rhythm
> Working you, slow mile by mile,
> Into your proper haunt
> Somewhere, well out, beyond . . .
> (*FW*, 24)

It is that proper haunt the poet seeks in this book: the area that is his by choice and not dictated by circumstance, for as he wrote in a 1972 essay, "Poetry is out of the quarrel with ourselves and the quarrel with others is rhetoric." The true poet, by definition, is a loner, a seeker of solitude, and Heaney must follow the example of his fisherman despite the potential cost.

Part of his proper haunt is art, and in this book he also writes of the passing of artists, notably composer Sean O'Riada and poet Robert Lowell, whose personal and artistic courage Heaney greatly admires:

> Lowell's bravery was different from the bravery of John Berryman or Sylvia Plath, with whom his name has often been joined. They swam powerfully into the dark swirls of the unconscious and the drift dowards death, but Lowell resisted that, held fast to conscience and pushed deliberately toward self-mastery. (*P,* 223–24)

The admiration of that bravery works its way into the poetry as well:

> No. You were our night ferry
> thudding in a big sea,
>
> the whole craft ringing
> with an armourer's music
> the course set wilfully across
> the ungovernable and dangerous.
> (*FW,* 32)

Heaney searches in *Field Work* for the courage to steer such a poetic course, to emulate the vision of Lowell, and even follows this poem, "Elegy," with an excellent sequence of sonnets written in Glanmore. (Indeed, all these poems were written outside Heaney's native ground, which may help explain his searching for a proper haunt.) Yet even in this poem the strength Heaney has found in his archaeological writings shines through what threatens to become a Lowellized verse.

Throughout his fifth book, in fact, Heaney's newly relaxed rhythms and diction (the reader will have far less recourse to the *Oxford English Dictionary* than in *North*) still echo with the clanging of Germanic consonants and Anglo-Saxon stress patterns. And so his interest in digging brings him back yet again to his starting point, but with a more mature awareness of his art, a more subtle phrasing than "I'll dig with it":

> Then I landed in the hedge school of Glanmore
> And from the backs of ditches hoped to raise
> A voice caught back off slug-horn and slow chanter
> That might continue, hold, dispel, appease:
> Vowels ploughed into other, opened ground,
> Each verse returning like the plough turned round.
> (*FW,* 34)

That marvelous image of the *boustrophedon,* the reversing of direction of every other line of writing—a common feature of ancient Greek poetry—Heaney pushes back to its root origin, "as the ox ploughs." There remains in his work a reaching back into tradition, both literary and linguistic, to reinvigorate our understanding of that tradition. The impact in his verse often arises from this jarring eruption of the past into the present, surprising readers into new awareness.

This passage, from the second of ten "Glanmore Sonnets," also points to a major source of the tension in *Field Work:* the struggle between normality and domesticity on the one hand and political awareness and engagement of the forces of history on the other. Much of the volume is taken up with poetry of family life and rural experience: the subjects of the early books, although from a more mature perspective. At the same time, however, the events in Ulster insinuate themselves into the poetry. In "The Badgers" the mysterious, ghostly passage of a badger through the garden becomes associated with "some violent shattered boy" looking for his lost youth. In another poem composer Sean O'Riada becomes "our jacobite / . . . our young pretender." *Field Work* tacitly acknowledges that one can only dwell directly on the violence in Northern Ireland for so long without turning from it and trying to make a normal life, a normal poetry. Yet even there one cannot leave it completely behind. From the first poem of the volume to the last, the public and political contend with the private and personal, neither ever fully gaining supremacy. That striving between rival forces often plays itself out in this volume as a suspicion of the poet's own motives, a self-criticism almost to the point of loathing.

In the first poem, for instance, "Oysters," the delight of eating oysters in a convivial setting runs headlong into images of the violence done to the oysters themselves, "Millions of them ripped and shucked and scattered" (*FW,* 11), and to a class-conscious image of the bivalves as a "Glut of privilege." The first stanza's richness of experience invokes auditory, visual, and gustatory sensations in the shells clacking and the taste conjuring up "starlight," the constellations Pleiades and Orion, and the saltiness of the ocean. Yet all this sensory joy gives way to images of violence, even rape, in the second stanza, as the oysters lie "Alive and violated / . . . on their beds of ice." The third stanza echoes the first in its emphasis on comradery and ease in the act of consumption, all the while laying a course for the fourth, in which the poet imagines the Romans packing oysters over the Alps in their pursuit of empire. Clearly, he associates privilege with the conquerors and, having spent his whole life seeing himself as one of the class of victims of imperialism, he finds himself in conflict with his own origins. In the final stanza, then, he fails to resolve this internal war, falling back first into anger at his inability to simply enjoy this simple repast and then into hope "that its tang / Might quicken me all into verb, pure verb." The poem becomes, then, a sort of prologue for the volume as a whole an attempt at creation by fiat, at turning the unresolved conflicts and turmoil of one's life into something realized, artistic, whole.

Yet elsewhere in the volume his attitude suggests that the purity of his art cannot save him. In "An Afterwards," for example, he imaginatively explores the hell for poets envisioned by his wife, who would "plunge" them all in the "ninth circle." Yet even in the midst of this torment, Heaney cannot resist (in the form of his future shade) inquiring of his wife as to which living poet is most revered on earth. The query draws an angry rebuke, as she accuses him of deserting the family for poetry, asking why he could not have

> "Unclenched, and come down laughing from your room
> And walked the twilight with me and the children—
> Like that one evening of elder bloom
> And hay, when the wild roses were fading?"
>
> (*FW*, 44)

His crime seems excessive seriousness more than anything else, an inability to take his eye off the prize even for something as intimate as family interaction. Indeed, the charge finds increased force in its particularity, aimed as it is at Heaney the rural, agrarian poet. Can it be true, we ask as we read, that he can write so brilliantly about the countryside and yet avoid it? Is poetry, then, a substitute for action, for life?

Yet the poem, filled as it is with humor, undercuts the charge; it unclenches even as it accuses him of remaining clenched. The poem is filled with whimsy, from the daisy-chain to the image of his wife delivering her tirade "as some maker gaffs me in the neck." Moreover, even as his wife accuses him, she also absolves him of a certain level of blame, noting that he "aspired to a kind, / Indifferent, faults-on-both-sides tact." While that acknowledgment sets him as not the worst among poets, it hardly qualifies as praise. Even here, however, the poem is making another reversal, for what appears acquittal turns out to be another indictment. The word "indifferent" suggests the poet's own fears that he has remained too aloof from events and involvements in his verse, that in attempting to be even-handed he has become bland, ineffectual.

This poem, then, points to two major concerns Heaney finds confronting him in this volume: first, that his poetry has failed to engage the political reality because it is so insistently fair-minded, so earnestly trying to understand the other side; and second, that a part of his personal life has slipped away, almost without his noticing, because he has been staring too fixedly at "larger questions." In a sense, both these questions arise out of a combination of his sense of moving into middle age and his newfound enthusiasm for Dante. The *Divine Comedy* stands as the preeminent work of middle age in Western culture, simultaneously considering life "In the middle of our way" and anticipating, exploring the next life. At the same time, it stakes out its political territory clearly, often savaging the poet's enemies, real or imagined, and rewriting history according to Dante's biases. Those propensities, along with the clear, unmuddied stance on every issue and personage in the poem, places Heaney in a clearly inferior position as he draws his comparisons. Yet he nevertheless invokes the *Comedy* throughout *Field Work,* and it will remain with him in subsequent works, as well.

The political realities call for treatment almost immediately in the volume. The second poem, the sequence "Triptych," begins with a poem about the aftermath of an assassination. The British Ambassador to Ireland, Christopher Ewart-Biggs, was murdered in July 1976. "After a Killing," as the title suggests, is concerned less with that murder than with conditions after it. Fulfilling our expectations, the opening stanza invokes two young men with rifles on the hill, waiting to kill. Yet the poem moves immediately beyond that image, "profane and bracing" as it may be, to ask who regrets the Irish predicament, "Who dreamt that we might dwell among ourselves / In rain and scoured light and wind-dried stones?" (*FW,* 12). One of the issues in the poem, as in the society, is the presence of outsiders, the constant reminder that the Northern Irish have been unable to dwell among themselves. As the poet attempts to tease out a vision adequate to the situation, the versification breaks down, until by the fourth stanza the prosody grinds to a halt under the burden of four full stops in the first two and a half lines. Clearly, the vatic function fails in handling the material, and it remains to ordinary reality to intercede on the poem's behalf:

> And today a girl walks in home to us
> Carrying a basket full of new potatoes,
> Three tight green cabbages, and carrots
> With the tops and mould still fresh on them.

This last quatrain accomplishes several functions at once. It points out to us that life goes on even in the face of atrocity, that on some level the waters of social forgetfulness close over even the important man's death. Moreover, it reasserts a kind of peasant Irish persistence: whatever may happen in the world at large, the rural Ireland of potatoes and nationalist green and good Irish mold will continue. And finally, the lines offer an almost pre-Raphaelite resolution, the exact depiction of a very small scene in the face of larger, insoluble questions. Yet Heaney suspects such a resolution and turns it into not the end of the poem but the leaping off point for its successor.

The third of the triptych, "At the Water's Edge," holds interest beyond its own merits as a sort of trial piece for the later "Station Island" sequence. In this poem Heaney visits three islands in Lough Erne in County Fermanagh. Devonish contains monastic ruins, Boa pre-Christian sculpture; between them he finds something like the history of Ireland in silent figures and elusive meanings (as the snipe's appearance, reminiscent of "The Backward Look," suggests). On Horse Island he finds a deserted hut and hears a maneuvering Army helicopter, which draws him in memory back to the protest march at Newry the week after Bloody Sunday. Certainly the sudden apparition of the past, the way the helicopter conjures "The scared, irrevocable steps" (*FW,* 14), anticipates the movement of poems in the later sequence, as does the setting on island ruins. Perhaps most significant, though, is the mood, the urge "to bow down, to offer up, / To go barefoot, foetal and penitential, / / And pray at the water's edge." The pull of memory and place on Heaney has always been strong, of course, and we can hear in this passage the same impulse he expresses in "The Tollund Man."

Yet at the same time this drive to pray is more vague: he would go to Aarhus to pray for certain eventualities, whereas in this poem he will simply "pray at the water's edge." The change in goals may signal a move from delving after solutions to wishing for spiritual wholeness, from youth's confidence in answers to middle age's desire for solace.

One means of achieving such healing is understanding, and in a poem like "The Badgers" he attempts to see how closely his own social and mental position approximates one very different. The badger, ghostly and disturbing in its nocturnal forays through the gardens, suggests to the poet not a mere victim but "some violent shattered boy," a terrorist, perhaps, hoist on his own petard. Heaney makes clear the connection between badgers and terrorists: they make their runs "under the night," make their presence known by the "carcasses" they leave in their wake, and "One that grew notorious / lay untouched in the roadside" (*FW,* 25). All of this is perhaps predictable enough. What fascinates, though, is the level of empathy the poet musters for these threatening and mysterious creatures. The badger, in fact, becomes emblematic of all that is alien to human experience in the old Romantic dichotomies: wilderness / civilization, chaos / order, dark / light, night / day, violence / peace. One might well envision him as associated with Satanic forces in a Hawthorne story. Even in Heaney's early work, the poet's younger self would likely recoil in panic from a creature of such primal force. Yet here, he recognizes the admirable qualities of strength and tenacity, right down to "The unquestionable houseboy's shoulders / that could have been my own" (*FW,* 26). That ability to find common ground with the Other has been present in Heaney's poetry at least since "The Tollund Man." He refuses to dismiss the badger, just as he does the terrorist with whom he associates it, as merely alien or frightening or evil. Heaney, then, demonstrates a kind of psychic health in his ability to connect something (himself) with something very different. In such a reading, the poem becomes a sort of political "Road Not Taken," hinting at the proximity of violence for any Northern Catholic, perhaps for any resident of modern Ulster, regardless of religion.

Still, the political is not the only realm of concern in *Field Work.* The book's form is much more open, much looser, much less self-concerned with its own unity than that of *North.* And more personal. Although Heaney has never been comfortable with the self-indulgence of the confessional mode in current poetry, he feels the pull of the personal and familial as material for his verse. For the success in using that material in this volume, much credit must go to Robert Lowell, from whom Heaney has learned, in Neil Corcoran's phrase, "that very artful combination of intent concentration and almost-inconsequentiality which . . . deflects confessional narcissism into an insouciant drama of self-perception."[1] Heaney can wring powerful emotion from personal situations without sliding into sentimentality or bathos in part because his treatment of them rarely exist for their own sakes or remain in that single plane.

At times he displaces personal unpleasantness or anxiety into the realm of imagination and dreams, the power of which not only drives "An Afterwards" but also informs much of the poetry in *Field Work.* The marital disharmony at the end of "A Dream of Jealousy" is no less for its being dreamt. In the dream the poet walks with his wife and a second, unidentified woman through a woodland setting, where nature seems to be urging on carnal thoughts. The "whispering grass / Ran its fingers through our guessing silence" (*FW,* 50). When the talk ranges over desire and jealousy, the speaker asks the other woman to reveal her "breast's mauve star" to him, which she does. The poet then discovers his erroneous judgment of the situation in his wife's injured look, 'O neither these verses / Nor my prudence, love, can heal your wounded stare." The damage is the more remarkable for the lack of action. As so often in his work, Heaney presents himself here as voyeur, asking not for sexual favors but only for a glimpse of their possibility. The poem works affectively by making us see the validity of the wife's response; while the situation may be imagined, that desire for otherness and propensity for inflicting hurt lie, with jealousy, just under the surface of our civil demeanors.

"High Summer" points in the other direction, ostensibly offering a glimpse into family life during the period covered in both "Summer Home" from *Winter Out* and "Summer 1969" from the "Singing School" sequence in *North.* The poem organizes itself around the baby's crying "inconsolably" at night while teething, the rhythms of rural life in the basque country, and the poet's fishing in the evenings. All of this is beautifully realized in a wealth of exact sensory detail. Yet these details, while creating a powerful sense of the experience itself, are but the leaping off point for the poem's conclusion, which is itself twofold. Preparing to leave, the poet opens a bag of maggots bought sometime earlier for fishing, and a mess of flies pours out, in a wonderfully precise oxymoron, "in a gauzy meaty flight" (*FW,* 46). He compares their course to a newsreel of a police force run amok," the sole reminder here of the rioting in Ulster that summer or to General Franco's Guardia Civil, both of which received greater play in the earlier poems. The thrust, instead, is on the transcendence of the images that close the poem. The flies, so marvelously vital, remind the poet that even neglected things reach maturity and that stunning transformations, miracles of sorts, take place every day. The teething child will one day be a man; while the poem insists on no such reading, the prominence given the crying child leads us, gently, to this conclusion.

That image in turn gives way to the poem's amazing closing lines: "We left by the high bare roads of the *pays basque* / where calvaries sentry the crossroads like masts / and slept that night near goatbells in the mists" (*FW,* 46). This ending astonishes on several levels all at once. The first and third lines stand as a lesson in what can be done with monosyllables, conveying in matter-of-fact, clean language a reality that borders on the magical. Sandwiched between them, the multisyllabic penultimate line with its falling rhythms—a dactyl and two trochees—points to the greater metrical equality of the one-syllable word lines. Moreover, the lines resonate in both similarity and contrast. The "bare roads" find fellow images in the bare crucifixes of the calvaries and the great bare road (the phrase sounds like one of Heaney's pet kennings in the eighth "Glanmore Sonnet"), the sea, invoked by the masts. Even the mists in the last line create a kind of bareness of view, obscuring the nearby goats, whose only evidence is auditory (their bells), not visual. The calvaries metamorphose into first crossroads and then masts, which for their part recall the bamboo fishing poles, a similarly serene image from earlier in the poem. Even the off-rhymes of *basque / masts / mists,* like the repeated *t*'s of the final line, contribute to the resonance. This closing, like the flies image before it, suggests the ways in which ordinary reality can be transmuted, altered, made to teach something deeper and full of wonder.

The poem's insistence on transformation holds implications for the poet's life as well. High summer, the poet's young adulthood, will soon give way to another season. Throughout the volume Heaney has scattered reminders that life is in a constant state of flux. The grown man writing an elegy for Francis Ledwidge was not long ago a child holding his Aunt Mary's hand. Friends who were here yesterday are dead today. Ledwidge himself died in "a big strafe" in both his (age twenty-eight) and the year's (July 31) high summer. The "Glanmore Sonnets" capture the rhythms of change in a rural setting, and of course, the frequent invoking of Dante reminds readers that the end is always near.

Yet perhaps nowhere does the book signal its anticipation of change to come than in the autumnal poems, "September Song," "Leavings," and "Harvest Bow." In language, imagery, and tone, these three poems insist that something has passed. "September Song" most resolutely situates us on the brink of change, from the first line's borrowing from Dante, "In the middle of our way," to the narrower gradation of the closing, in which "We toe the line / between the tree in leaf and the bare tree" (*FW,* 43). The poem's occasion is the immanent move away from Glanmore, itself a moment of transition, of leaving behind a settled and, to judge by the "Sonnets," a happy time for something less certain, if more lucrative financially. Even this choice of subject matter reinforces the poem's thematic thrust, as does the setting in September, when the "fern subsides" and "acorns / shine from the grassy verges," this last word is a brilliant double entendre. It is a time of both ripeness and loss.

While they focus less on that impermanence, both "Leavings" and "The Harvest Bow" employ the same end-of-summer half-season. In "The Harvest Bow" the title object, tied by his father, reminds Heaney of time slipping away and of the frailty of his own art. The bow is a perfect emblem for the elder Heaney in its rural ties and its silence (which the poet mentions whenever his father appears in his verse). Like that more famous "foster child of silence and slow time," Keats's Grecian urn, the bow attains a motto, "*The end of art is peace.*" Yet Heaney asserts it less confidently than does Keats, suggesting only that it "Could be the motto of this frail device." Even so, the bow holds implications for Heaney's own art. The self-sufficiency, completeness, and tranquility embodied by the harvest bow compare favorably with Heaney's poetry, which requires a reader to be completed and a reader's approval to be successful. In "Leavings" the political and the seasonal are more overtly connected. The burning of the barley stubble leads Heaney to think of the stained glass windows of the Catholic churches that were "threshed clear by Thomas Cromwell" (*FW,* 57). Again borrowing from Dante, the poet wonders which circle of hell Cromwell inhabits, walking on burning cobblestones, "each one a broken statue's head." Still, the thrust of the poem is not wholly political, and Heaney moves on to envision a nocturnal stroll through the smoldering fields, where one would encounter the ghost of Will Brangwen, the father in D. H. Lawrence's great novel of the rhythms of life and the passing of generations, *The Rainbow.* The ghost becomes the occasion for a celebration of pure sound in the poem's closing, in which he is described as "a breaking sheaf of light, / abroad in the hiss / and clash of stooking." The lines are an almost perfect rendering of the "soft whoosh" of steaming barley straw after a fire. Moreover, they serve to remind us, in a volume so taken up with current events and historical consciousness, that the purpose, after all, is not journalism but poetry. This final image is something like the "pure verb" he hopes the oysters of the opening poem may quicken him into, and throughout the volume, there are moments like this one, in which the subject is language itself and what it can be made to do.

As befits a book with such a strong sense of being poised on the brink, *Field Work* has not one but two focal points, standing Janus-like with one eye on life and one on death. The former center is comprised chiefly of the "Glanmore Sonnets" and the title sequence; the latter by the six elegies and remembrances. The twin opposed tendencies represented by the two groups threatens at times to pull the book apart, yet the placement—with the elegies coming in the first half the book, subsequently balanced by the sonnets—suggests a resolution of sorts. Maybe, the book's structure suggests, life goes on even in the face of death.

The six elegiac poems divide evenly between artists with whom Heaney has some connection and friends or relatives killed in the Troubles. Of the six, "Elegy," for Robert Lowell, is probably the least convincing. Heaney always seems least sure of himself when writing about other writers, and writing an elegy about the "master elegist," as he calls Lowell, causes special difficulties. He finds further trouble in achieving a linguistic level adequate to the masculine, powerful language of Lowell, and so lapses into a false bravado.

Heaney is on more solid footing in his memorial poems for Sean O'Riada and Francis Ledwidge, in part because he knows why he is writing about them. O'Riada, the composer and conductor who died in 1971 at age forty, was not only a friend of the poet's, but he also offered Ulster a certain level of cultural legitimacy. Heaney uses the poem to explore the connection between art and politics. O'Riada, the Jacobite, the specifically Catholic pretender, herds his orchestra *south,* toward the Republic, where the arts have a history of greater standing. The poem also invokes Yeats, the great poet of Irish nationalism, in describing the composer as

> more falconer than fisherman, I'd say,
> unhooding a sceptic eye

> to greet the mackerel's barred cold,
> to pry whatever the cuckoo called.
> (*FW*, 29)

It is no mean feat to allude, in a single quatrain, to "The Second Coming," "The Fisherman," and "Under Ben Bulben," yet Heaney manages. The poem does not attempt to suggest that O'Riada's work is somehow overtly nationalistic, nor is any mention made of the man's own political views. Rather, it suggests that the composer became public property, the focal point for the community's needs, simply because of his prominence in a field of public, artistic endeavor; not a young pretender but *our* young pretender, *our* Jacobite. In this sense, O'Riada becomes a release point for the pressures the poet feels to "say something" or "do something" about the "situation in Ulster." Each of Heaney's books has been criticized from some quarter or other for the way it deals or fails to deal with political events. This poem shows him on the other side of the transaction, as part of the community desirous of a leader, a representative, a symbol.

Francis Ledwidge presents a clearer study in politics and history, and the memorial poem to him fully addresses the questions his death raises. Many promising artists died in the Great War, including many more talented than Ledwidge, who was a lesser talent than either Edward Thomas or Wilfred Owen. Yet his level of achievement is beside the point; rather, what makes him such an interesting figure for Heaney is his ambivalence toward the project, precisely the attitude presented by Yeat's Irish airman. Heaney handles the subject matter quite differently, though. Whereas Yeats's poem is all heroism and lonely nobility, Heaney's is chiefly Irish domesticity. The war scenes are uniformly passive—Ledwidge "Ghosting the trenches," sucking on stones to make his mouth water, even dying passive, "rent / By shrapnel" (*FW*, 60)—as quiet as the bronze soldier that frames the poem. The memorial statue, seen by the young Heaney shortly after World War II on excursion with his Aunt Mary, presents the typically heroic, stiff representation of the soldier: his cape "crumple[d] stiffly in an imagined wind / No matter how the real winds buff and sweep / His sudden hunkering run." The whole point of the poem is that Ledwidge was anything but a typical soldier. While he may have worn the uniform of a Tommy, his "haunted Catholic face, pallid and brave" sets him off from his fellow soldiers. Stanzas 6 and 7 picture him courting by the sea not far from Slane, County Meath, "where you belonged."

Later, the poet sees him in the trenches with a "silence cored from a Boyne passage-grave." The trenches are themselves a kind of passage-grave, and the phrase anticipates Ledwidge's death. Moreover, it marks him again as belonging in the Boyne valley, not in Flanders and not in the British army.

The whole question of belonging permeates the poem. The child Heaney belongs to his Aunt Mary, a "worried pet" with a tight grip on her hand. There is subsequently news of a large litter with the decision to "pet the runt." The poem quotes Ledwidge as belonging to the Irish countryside, a British subject fulfilling a duty of questionable authenticity "while my country / Has no place among nations." The regularity of the form of the poem, with its iambic pentameter and *a b a b* quatrains, reminds the reader that the lyric form is also a British subject, and that poetry necessarily implicates an Irish writer in the historical morass that dragged Ledwidge, like Robert Gregory, to an ambivalent death: "You were not keyed or pitched like these true-blue ones / Though all of you consort now underground." This curious figure, "our dead enigma," is not nearly so resolute as "this vigilant bronze," and his example reminds the poet of those other names on the plaque who died fighting for England, while their countrymen died fighting against it. The awkwardness and complexity of the situation is worthy of Dante, and Heaney follows the poem with his translation of the Ugolino cantos.

There are more recent deaths, of course, that call the political situation into more immediate question, and he deals with three of these in separate elegies. The victims come from different backgrounds and represent various elements of the tragedy that is recent Northern Irish history. Colum McCartney, a cousin of Heaney's and a farmer, is the subject of "The Strand at Lough Beg." Sean Armstrong, of "A Postcard from North Antrim," was a friend of Heaney's from university and a Belfast social worker. Although unnamed in "Casualty," Louis O'Neill, in some ways the most interesting and compelling figure, was one of the fishermen in "A Lough Neagh Sequence" and a frequenter of many pubs, including the one run by Heaney's father-in-law. The three poems, while each distinct from the others, share some common territory. In each case, the murder itself is taken care of by the midpoint, so that Heaney can use the remainder of the poem to meditate on the meaning of the man's life and death. In proper spirit for elegies, the deaths are not the ending but the starting points. And in each case, as in Joyce's "The Dead" or in Dante, the men seem more alive than dead. Heaney enjoins Armstrong to get up off the floor and wipe away the blood, so inconceivable is it that he's dead. In "A Postcard from North Antrim" and "Casualty" he abandons the pentameter of the bulk of the book and reverts to the shorter line and freer metrics of *North.* And in all three cases, the old terseness fights against any strains of sentimentality that try to insinuate their way into the verse.

'The Strand at Lough Beg" is the most nearly classical elegy of the three, or at least the most aware of the classical tradition. Rather than following the elegiac tradition, it takes many of those conventions and stands them on their head. For instance, in the classical elegy all nature mourns the lost shepherd. Yet in this poem Colum McCartney's cattle "turn their unbewildered gaze" to watch Heaney and McCartney's ghost make their way through the foggy pasture, where "Lough Beg half shines under the haze" (*FW,* 18). In the classical elegy both speaker and deceased are depicted as shepherds. Here, they are shown among the cattle, yet without the nobility of the tradition: "Big-voiced scullions, herders, feelers round / Haycocks and hindquarters, talkers in byres, / Slow arbitrators of the burial ground." These farmers are literal, unromanticized, ordinary. They display the usual Heaney reticence, people who "fought shy, / Spoke an old language of conspirators / And could not crack the whip or seize the day." The passage points to the new type of conspirator, of whom McCartney is a victim, who is quite capable of cracking the whip and seizing the day. McCartney is pictured as peaceful, frightened even of the spent shells of the duck hunters. While there is not contemplation of divine justice or mercy in this elegy, the poem does examine worldly evils. And finally, the speaker does decorate the bier, in a passage borrowed from the *Purgatorio:* "With rushes that shoot green again, I plait / Green scapulars to wear over your shroud."

The poem also utilizes the tripartite structure of the ode. The first section sets the scene and witnesses the murder. The second moves back to discuss McCartney's ill-suitedness for the world of terrorists. The third, then, offers the dream sequence of the two men moving across the farm, McCartney falling, and Heaney washing him with dew and moss.

If Heaney elects not to portray his cousin's murder in journalistic detail, it is not because he misperceives the nature of violence, nor that he blanches in its presence. A reading of *North* or *Sweeney Astray* is ample to prove that point. Rather, to present McCartney as he really was would be to sensationalize the poem, to detract from the poem's thematic and aesthetic purposes and turn instead toward propaganda. The poem, after all, seeks to be elegiac, not incendiary.

He faces up to the act of violence more directly in "Casualty," perhaps because the issue of the victim's culpability clouds the question of blame. Colum McCartney's only apparent mistake is driving away from the safety of his home community. In Louis O'Neill, on the other hand, Heaney finds someone who knowingly and wilfully violates "Our tribe's complicity" by going out drinking during the curfew after Bloody Sunday. In fact, from the first, O'Neill is established as a man with little regard for the social niceties. A solitary drinker, he orders his drinks silently through slight hand gestures. At closing time he leaves by himself. Even his business is solitary, for he is one of the Lough Neagh fishermen, poaching eels for which a British fishing company holds the rights. He's "A dole-kept breadwinner / But a natural for work" (*FW,* 21). O'Neill is cagey, cautious, "Sure-footed but too sly." With the regular *a b a b c d c d* rhyme scheme and the trimeter—although Heaney takes great liberties with the meter—this figure suddenly becomes oddly familiar, the contemporary version of Yeats's fisherman in the poem of that title, now unidealized, unherioc. Still, Heaney has set himself a great challenge: can he write for this man, or his memory, one poem "as cold and passionate as the dawn"?

Part 2 begins with a recounting of the funeral for the thirteen dead men, with its air of unreality, the coffins seeming to float out of the cathedral. The event offers a tremendous communal bond, locking all members together, "braced and bound." All except one. O'Neill's refusal to obey a curfew imposed by "his own crowd" leads to his being in the distant pub when the bomb explodes, "Remorse fused with terror / In his still knowable face." This last is a brilliant phrase, conjuring up the awful aftermath and at the same time insisting that the face stays with the poet in memory—it is still knowable, even after the blast that destroyed it. That he would go out drinking was a given, the next stanza tells us, and asks to what extent he was responsible for his own murder:

"Now you're supposed to be
An educated man,"
I hear him say, "Puzzle me
    The right answer to that one."
(*FW,* 23)

Indeed, O'Neill's life and death form a challenge for Heaney: Can his "tentative art" understand, let alone make itself understandable to, one whose back (we're shown his back three times) is so resolutely turned to custom and social order? Unwilling or unable to engage the fisherman in the realm of poetry, Heaney is marginally more successful at entering the other's realm, the world of public houses and fishing boats.

Stanza 3 closes the poem with a rumination on the kind of freedom the fisherman enjoyed, as the purr of the hearse at his funeral (which Heaney missed) metamorphoses into the fishing boat at trolling speed. Heaney remembers the morning he went out on the boat, although he acknowledges that he only "tasted freedom." As the poem has shown, such freedom can carry a terrible risk with it. Yet it also brings joy

> As you find a rhythm
> Working you, slow mile by mile,
> Into your proper haunt
> Somewhere, well-out, beyond . . .
> (*FW,* 24)

The effect of the last line, with its three spondees (or near spondee, in the case of "beyond"), is to stop the flow of the poem completely. This revery, attractive as it is for the poet, cannot continue. Heaney has worked himself well out into his proper haunt, to the point where he is ready to take on Yeats: "Dawn-sniffing revenant, / Plodder of the midnight rain, / Question me again." This is the sort of rhetorical flourish Yeats would employ, as he does at the end of "Among School Children" or "Under Ben Bulben." In Heaney's case it is redundant, since the very memory of O'Neill poses the question for him. The poem proves worthy of its formal bravado; Heaney succeeds in mixing passion and a cold eye, emotion and moral judgment. This is one of the great elegies, indeed one of the great poems, of contemporary verse.

Yet to give too much weight to the elegies, as spectacular as they are, is to falsify the thrust of *Field Work,* for the book is about life as well as death. One of its achievements is to celebrate married life and love. The series of poems including "The Otter," "The Skunk," "Homecomings," and "Field Work" offers a delightful array of erotic moments and images. The title figure in "The Otter," surprisingly, is the beloved, the female, diving and splashing, swimming on her back with "silent, thigh-shaking kick" in the pool of "My two hands" (*FW,* 47).

Or perhaps it is not surprising, given the poet's fear of water, already mentioned in "Elegy," and his penchant for portraying himself as voyeur. "Homecomings" is even more overtly erotic. The sandmartin, which skims "breast to breast with himself" (*FW,* 49) over the river, flies into "the worn mouth of the hole" and "kisse[s] home." Meanwhile, the water near the nest is "lipping the bank." In the fourth and final numbered quatrain, the poet becomes the sandmartin, seeking his erotic nest:

> Mould my shoulders inward to you.
> Occlude me.
> Be damp clay pouting.
> Let me listen under your eaves.

The lover's desire to be hidden away in his beloved is conventional enough, but Heaney's use of the sandmartin as the emblem of that desire invigorates and charges the metaphor.

Similarly, the imperfection of the vaccination mark on his wife's thigh becomes a mark of desire in "Field Work," transformed into a host of natural images—a chestnut, a scar on a tree's bark, a sunflower—ultimately giving way in the fourth poem to an erotic ritual of staining her hand with a leaf from a flowering currant. What these poems variously suggest are the manifold ways in which the lover can find emblems of his desire in nature and the delight to be found in mature, erotic love. This is a Heaney not seen before, not even in the erotic homages to the female bog people, for he expresses a tenderness as well as a need that his highly masculine verse has not heretofore acknowledged.

The "Glanmore Sonnets" represent a particularly notable step in Heaney's poetic development, given the violence done to the English poetic line in *Wintering Out* and *North.* Here is the poet of the half-line and ringing alliteration, the stanza-as-archaeological-instrument, suddenly offering up the most conventional form of lyric poem. The undertaking entails considerable risk on his part, for Heaney has never fully mastered iambic pentameter, has never seemed fully comfortable—student of Hopkins, Hughes, and Anglo-Saxon verse—with the completely regular line. Yet that weakness, if weakness it be, he transforms in these sonnets into a positive strategy, as we can see in the opening lines of the seventh sonnet:

> Dogger, Rockall, Malin, Irish Sea:
> Green, swift upsurges, North Atlantic flux
> Conjured by that strong gale-warning voice
> Collapse into a sibilant penumbra.
> (*FW*, 39)

Clearly, this is a less regular metric than the one informing

> That time of year thou mayest in me behold
> When yellow leaves, or none, or few, do hang
> Upon those boughs which shake against the cold,
> Bare ruined choirs where late the sweet birds sang.

Yet the two poems have something of the same sentiment, that changes of the seasons, in Shakespeare, of weather, in Heaney, as metaphorical equivalents for human states of being. The differences are chiefly formal. The modern sonnet takes greater liberties with metrics, the four lines containing five, six (I would give swift its own beat), five, and four beats. Moreover, the first two lines defy conventional scansion. Heaney's opening line, trochaic with a caesura after each metrical foot, utterly blocks any sense of progress or flow. The self-contained metrical feet, separated from one another by caesurae, emphasize the violence of the storm, which we might well expect to throw the ships onto the rocks.

Such is not the case, however, for the sirens wail "And drive the trawlers to the lee of Wicklow." And to a fully conventional scansion, one might observe. The metrics reflect the greater safety offered by the sheltered bay. While the way of organic form is fraught with peril, the strategy here permits Heaney to employ his own approach to prosody within the conventions of the sonnet, and at a certain level the poem is about the melding of those disparate traditions. When the poet looks upon the bay and utters the words "A haven," the narrative thread follows the course of the word itself, as it brightens, "deepening, clearing, like the sky," out above other islands in the North Atlantic. This poem brings together the Old English lyric conventions, represented by the sea kennings and the Danish islands, with the conventions of the English lyric after the Renaissance, as represented by the sonnet itself. The result is at best an uneasy cessation of hostilities. Even the rhyme scheme of the sestet, matching up *Helene* / bay / marvelous with haven / sky / Faroes manifests the distance the poet is putting between himself and the sonnet of Wordsworth, Shakespeare, and Donne. The rhymes of Shakespeare's Sonnet 73, by the way, are decay / uphold / cold / know / so. Similarly, in the couplet of the sixth sonnet, Heaney rhymes "goose" and "house," a sly acknowledgment of the origin of Ulster (Planter) English, for only a dialect derived from Lowland Scots, like that of the Ulster Protestants or the Canadians (like Ann Saddlemeyer, perhaps), pronounces "house" to rhyme with "goose." In each case, Heaney must make his own way, rather than writing in purely received forms.

Certainly the construction of a sonnet sequence in and of itself involves a statement about the poet's relation to the tradition, and the "Glanmore Sonnets" turn out to be an extremely literary exercise. In the first one, the penultimate line, anticipating the "Station Island" sequence six years later, declares that "My ghosts come striding into their spring stations" (*FW,* 33), and indeed, the sequence is filled with his ghosts. The sonnets reverse the move of one of Heaney's chief enduring ghosts, Patrick Kavanagh, in his sonnet sequence, "Temptation in Harvest." In it Kavanagh details a move from rural Monaghan to Dublin. Here, Heaney details a move from Dublin to rural Wicklow; and whereas Kavanagh describes a kind of loss, Heaney, who has frequently described himself as an Antaeus figure, rediscovers a strength in the firmer ground. He celebrates life close to nature, from the mist over the furrows to the rat staring in the window. Elsewhere, he recalls Joyce in the phrase "tart-leafed as inwit" (sonnet 9); Sir Thomas Wyatt, the father of the English sonnet, in the question from sonnet 10, "How like you this?," which he borrows from "They Flee from Me"; *The Merchant of Venice* in the reference to the eloping lovers, Lorenzo and Jessica, whose image is yoked to that of a Celtic equivalent pair, Diarmuid and Grainne; Boris Pasternak's "Hamlet" poem from *Dr. Zhivago* in the line "Now the good life could be to cross a field" in the opening sonnet.[2] Corcoran even makes a strong argument for Osip Mandelstam, whom Heaney clearly admires, as a "hidden presence" in the sequence, informing the sense of connection between nature and poetry. Yet I believe that Heaney is fully capable of arriving at the "Glanmore Sonnets" without Mandelstam and that his admiration for the Russian's work is a matter of finding ratification for his own poetics.

Beyond all these, however, the presiding genius of the sonnets is Wordsworth. No one can write a poem in English that celebrates the rural, the rustic, the simple without being to a greater or lesser degree in Wordsworth's debt, and Heaney here acknowledges his indebtedness. Some of the references and borrowings are explicit. In sonnet 3 he begins to compare "this strange loneliness" at Glanmore to Wordsworth and his sister, Dorothy. The opening line of sonnet 6, "He lived there in the unsayable lights," is an almost direct transcription of the famous Lucy poem, "She dwelt among the untrodden ways." The opening of sonnet 2, "Sensings, mountings from the hiding places," recalls *The Prelude's* "the hiding places of my power." Other borrowings are more formal than direct. As Corcoran notes, sonnets 4, 5, and 6 build on Wordsworthian "spots of time."[3] In sonnet 4 Heaney recalls listening to the railroad track for the sound of the oncoming train. The following poem situates an early sexual experience by an elderberry tree, "the boortree," which led him to become "etymologist of roots and graftings. In sonnet 6 the story from his childhood of the man "who dared the ice" points to a fascination with a certain kind of risk-taking in both life and literature. Yet Heaney gives each of these moments his own particular spin. They become neither mere occasions for nostalgia nor explanations of the poet's development, as they too often are in *Stations,* but metapoetic moments involved in their own creation. The erotic play of "touching tongues" in sonnet 5 extends beyond the sensual delight in tactile sensation of another's tongue to suggest the almost erotic charge in writing poetry—another way of touching someone else with one's tongue—as well as the nature of the intimacy of the poet–reader relationship. The child with his ear to the rail, listening for the message he can only infer from the ripples in his drinking glass, comes to symbolize the poet's search for the ephemeral lying behind the quotidian and the concrete. Indeeed, as he explains in sonnet 2, that search comprises the whole mystery of art and works in two directions. In that sonnet he relates Oisin Kelly's tale of trying to find rather than create the sculpture: "hankering after stone / That connived with chisel, as if the grain / Remembered what the mallet tapped to know" (*FW,* 34). Not surprisingly, then, the sequence that so delights in its allusiveness and erudition, that revels in its own creative process, is simultaneously an act of drawing the poem out of the place and a rumination on that act. Heaney, a relatively conservative poet formally, shows himself to be quite in touch with postmodern trends of reflexivism and self-referentiality. Of course, in his case, that metalanguage may be as much in the spirit of Donne and Marvell as of Borges and Fowles.

Yet the game never becomes its own goal in the "Glanmore Sonnets"; the ostensible subject matter really does matter. Sonnet 9 offers the bay tree by the gate (already mentioned in "Elegy") and the question of the poet's apology for poetry. At the same time, it remains concerned with the black rat swinging on a briar outside the kitchen window that frightens the poet's wife, as well as his own memory of rats killed during threshing. And in a sense it exists for its final two images, the empty swaying briar and his wife's face, which "Haunts like a new moon glimpsed through tangled glass" (*FW,* 41). The sonnets examine marriage in a new setting, celebrating especially mature married desire. In Sonnet 7 the thunderstorm evokes a host of portentous images and culminates in his desperate plea: "Come to me quick, I am upstairs shaking. / My all of you birchwood in lightning" (*FW,* 41). "My all of you" is a brilliant phrasing of erotic longing, worthy of the metaphysical poets in its double possessive, in which each pronoun is given over to the other. And Sonnet 10, with its allusion to Wyatt's famous lovers' scene, imagines husband and wife, who have retreated in fact to Glanmore, first in dream fleeing to Donegal to a love embrace in the moss and then in memory having escaped to their wedding night,

> When you came with your deliberate kiss
> To raise us towards the lovely and painful
> Covenants of flesh; our separateness;
> The respite in our dewy dreaming faces.
> (*FW,* 42)

There are few erotic moments in English more tender or more touching; once again, Heaney has dared to invoke a master, in this case Wyatt, and once again he has proved himself worthy of the comparison. He brilliantly conveys first the conjoining of the lovers in the two and a half lines unbroken by punctuation, and then the unbridgeable distance between them through the twin semicolons. In a sequence notable in large measure for the liberties taken with sonnet form and meter, the final line is one of the most regular, and most beautiful, he has ever written.

Part nature poetry, part poetry of flight from the Troubles, part metapoetry, part love poetry, the "Glanmore Sonnets" take all of their elements equally seriously. They affirm, in a time that can require so many elegies, that life is more than death, that there are places of peace, that hate and vengeance may noy be the only possible ruling passions, that love exists.

Chapter Six

Returning to Earth: The Sweeney Poems

It may be that every modern literature finds itself confronted by a set of cultural hurdles and expectations to be met and overcome, as well as literary forerunners in whose shadow writers must toil. Irish literature, of course, is dominated by the twin figures of its resident giants, Yeats and Joyce, and even they have felt the pressure of one of the liveliest bodies of mythology and legend in all Europe. Yeats gave over a great part of his life to retelling the tales of heroic Ireland, the Celtic Twilight that has been so influential in Irish writing and thinking ever since. Joyce tinkered with traditional literature and mythology in his novels, particularly in his use of Finn McCool in *Finnegans Wake.* More recently, Thomas Kinsella has translated the *Tain* as well as shorter lyrics.

On this point as on so many others, Heaney has gone his own way, choosing not some epic of heroic action but the more meditative, plaintive, and melancholy tale of scapegoating and alienation, *Buile Suibhne.* Both in his translation, *Sweeney Astray,* and in the "Sweeney Redivivus" section of *Station Island,* he strives to give Sweeney new life and to make him the poet's own. This effort stands as the third major use of the medieval work in this century. The first, a scholarly translation and commentary by J. G. O'Keeffe in 1910, was undertaken for the Irish Texts Society. In the second, altogether more sly, the journalist, novelist, and satirist Flann O'Brien employed the poem as an instrumental part of his novel *At Swim-Two-Birds. Sweeney Astray,* however, stands as the first translation of the poem by a major poet.

The story, as Heaney notes, is entirely literary rather than part of the longer tradition of Irish myth, as in the cases of Cuchulain or Finn McCool. There was a historical Suibhne Geilt, a minor king, what we would think of as a nobleman, whom O'Keeffe identifies as having fallen at the battle of Magh Rath. Yet beyond the name, the tale is in no respect concerned with the historical Suibhne. Rather, it takes this obscure figure, who is not even mentioned in all accounts of the battle,[1] and pushes him into an even more peripheral situation. Sweeney offends the cleric Ronan Finn repeatedly, first by casting his psalter to the bottom of a lake, where it is retrieved, miraculously unharmed, a day and a night later by an otter, who returns it to Ronan. Later, at the battle at Moira (the spellings here are consistent with modern usage and with Heaney's, rather than O'Keeffe's, translation) in what is now northwest County Down, Sweeney throws a spear, killing Ronan's assistant, as well as a second, which fails to kill the cleric himself only because it breaks his bell. Ronan utters very nearly the same curse after each of these two transgressions, right down to sparing Sweeney's wife, Eorann, for her attempt to restrain her fiery husband. In each case, Sweeney is cursed to roam the countryside, naked and mad, and to die at spear-point. Only in the second transgression is he also cursed with the change in form to a bird-man. During the battle, then, he is indeed driven mad and sent literally flying off to roam Ireland.

The remainder of the poem is an account of his misadventures in his madness and alienation: shunned and hunted by humans, ill-at-ease in his second home in the trees, always suspicious and wary, cold and ill-fed, ultimately reconciled to God and the Church. O'Keeffe argues this last element may well be a later emendation, that the madness in the earliest versions may have been due to the horrors of battle, and that the introduction of St. Ronan and St. Moling may represent the transformation of a pagan entertainment into a Christian cautionary tale. Whatever the ultimate truth, we may be sure that the text passed through a number of shaping hands; the result is something less than a seamless entity. As O'Keeffe notes, there are two separate intervals in the current tale in which Sweeney's madness abates, and they appear to be completely independent and ignorant of one another.[2] There are numerous repetitions of scenes and speeches, and even two versions of Sweeney's death.

The work is written, like so many early Irish works, in a mix of prose and poetry, the prose for exposition and general narration, the verse for heightened moments, descriptions, Sweeney's thoughts and observations. Heaney maintains these conventions, although he also takes liberties. For instance, in section 11, he turns the account of Sweeney's initial attack of madness and flight from battle from the original prose to verse. His greater change, however, is toward a modern melancholy and anxiety, in which the bird-man in his exile becomes a familiar image: "Insofar as Sweeney is also a figure of the artist, displaced, guilty, assuaging himself by his utterance, it is possible to read the work as an aspect of the quarrel between free creative imagination and the constraints of religious, political, and domestic obligation."[3] Perhaps—but what seems more likely is that if one is seeking such a figure, Sweeney will stand as well as the next. Clearly, though, Heaney has pushed his version of Sweeney in that direction, both in the poem and in the "glosses" in *Station Island.* That the poet feels a common bond with his character may be more instructive about the nature of the poet's "exile" than about the original tale; still, the empathy is real and heartfelt, and Sweeney provides Heaney with a desirable element in his poetic mixture.

Heaney's version is, on the whole, quite faithful to the original text. As he states in his introduction, the omissions in his translation are limited to a handful of passages. He shows remarkable restraint, for instance, in cutting only seven stanzas from the very lengthy section 40, in which Sweeney praises the trees of Ireland. Even so, certain changes are curious. For example, in section 43, in which Sweeney curses the woman picking watercress and thereby robbing him of his supper, Heaney drops the ultimate stanza, in which he extends the curse to Lynchseachan, his half-brother or foster-brother who tries repeatedly (succeeding once) to capture him. At times prose is changed to verse, although never, I believe vice versa. And at numerous points the tone or mood shifts, so that Heaney's mad king is, finally, more sorrowful and angst-ridden than O'Keeffe's. The major changes, though, lie in the realm of prosody. Rather than attempt to reproduce the poem's Gaelic conventions in English, as O'Keeffe and even O'Brien have done, Heaney renders passages into language and forms much closer to his own personal style. This strategy seems entirely to the point, for O'Keeffe's translation, while strictly faithful to the text, is often virtually unreadable. Heaney possesses a clearly superior ear, and merely to translate verbatim without bringing the tale any closer to modern readers would be a waste of his poetic gifts. Ciaran Carson has noted the changes in prosody in section 11, in which Heaney sacrifices the alliteration and assonance of the original, along with the rolling rhythm it achieves through its constant punctuation with "ands."[4] Still, Heaney's version, in verse, finds its own form of inner play:

> His brain convulsed,
> his mind split open.
> Vertigo, hysteria, lurchings

and launchings came over him,
he staggered and flapped desperately,
he was revolted by the thought of known places
and dreamed strange migrations.
His fingers stiffened,
his feet scuffled and flurried,
his heart was startled,
his senses were mesmerized,
his sight was bent,
the weapons fell from his hands
and he levitated in a frantic cumbersome motion
like a bird of the air.
And Ronan's curse was fulfilled.

(*SA*, 9)

The passage plays its own music, and Heaney has his own fun with outrageous anachronisms like "mesmerized," a nineteenth-century coinage.

Still, this version conveys everything either O'Keeffe's or O'Brien's version does, while pointing toward a different sense of the character. Carson complains about the introduction of "twentieth-century *angst*" that is unwarranted by the original,[5] yet this is a product not only of the medieval text but of the translator's vision, as Heaney freely admits:

It's not translated by me from an original in a new way. What I was doing was taking a parallel text and trying to turn it into a readable verse that was in my voice. I didn't deliberately set out to Heaneyize the text, certainly not. Here and there I did let go of it. . . . It is not a crib in any sense. On the other hand, having said that, it does not depart from the sense quatrain by quatrain.

Still, those quatrains bear the Heaney imprint. Ignoring the rigid prosodic rules of the original text, he writes his short line stanzas chiefly in the manner of *Wintering Out* or *North*. Compare, for instance, these stanzas:

O alder, thou art not hostile,
delightful is they hue,
thou art not rending and prickling
in the gap wherein thou art.

O little blackthorn, little thorny one;
O little black sloe tree;

O watercress, little green-topped one,
from the brink of the ousel spring.[6]

and

The alder is my darling,
all thornless in the gap,
some milk of human kindness
coursing in its sap.

The blackthorn is a jaggy creel
stippled with dark sloes;
green watercress in thatch on wells
where the drinking blackbird goes.
(*SA*, 37)

The overall sense is the same in the two passages, yet clearly the second offers greater euphony. It is also characteristically Heaney's. The word choices—the "jaggy creel" especially—mark the passage as his. Indeed, he identifies the first twelve or so stanzas as not a direct translation at all but "a poem of mine on the trees."

Another attractive element appears to be the encounter with hostile or opposed forces in the poem. From the outset, Sweeney comes into violent contact with others, and that pattern continues after his transformation, although his position shifts from aggressor to victim or quarry. In his exiled state, he is pursued by Lynchseachan and the mill hag, and he has a moving encounter with his wife, Eorann. In the case of each of the conflicts, Sweeney finds himself betrayed by someone he might hope to trust. Eorann is his wife, Lynchseachan his half-brother. Even the hag, in Heaney's hands, becomes something like the "poor old woman," that representative of Ireland, run amok. And in the moments when Sweeney is lucid, Ronan is beseeching God to make him mad again. The army chases him, and strangers and friends alike set traps to capture him, although their reasons remain obscure. Seemingly everything Irish conspires against him. Only the birds and his fellow madmen accept him—in particular a British madman named Alan. This easy alliance offers a happy coincidence for an Ulsterman translating the poem in the 1980s, for it suggests a historical linking of Britain, especially Scotland, and Ulster that predates the Battle of the Boyne by a thousand years.

Some of the conflicts, of course, are internal, or at least, related to his madness. In sections 64 and 65 the poem tells of Sweeney being pursued through the Fews by an apparition of headless torsos and disembodied heads. It was along this same road, we are told in *Field Work,* that Colum McCartney, the poet's cousin, was murdered by figures whose heads were hidden. Section 65 is another intense moment that Heaney elevates from its prose original to verse:

The heads were pursuing him,
lolling and baying,
snapping and yelping,
whining and squealing.
They nosed at his calves and his thighs,
they breathed on his shoulder,
they nuzzled the back of his neck,
they went bumping off tree-trunks and rock-face,
they spouted and plunged like a waterfall,
until he gave them the slip and escaped
in a swirling tongue of low cloud.
(*SA,* 69–70)

Even here, Sweeney is a madman of language and tongues, a true representative of the poet. More important, it is a tongue of low cloud, like the ground fog across the strand where Heaney has his vision, drawn from Dante, of his cousin falling in "The Strand at Lough Beg." In O'Keeffe's version Sweeney escapes into "filmy clouds of the sky." The change is evidently inspired by an impulse toward self-referentiality.

Yet perhaps the greatest appeal is the poem's celebration of nature and landscape. In an essay entitled, significantly, "The God in the Tree: Early Irish Nature Poetry," Heaney remarks that few poets in English can impart the same wonder and delight in nature that is a regular feature of early Irish nature poetry, which "registers certain sensations and makes a springwater music out of certain feelings in a way unmatched in any other European language" (*P,* 182). What he alludes to is the direct perception and description of nature without the classical or romantic filters through which it has been viewed in nearly all poetry—certainly in English poetry—since the early Renaissance. The essay goes on to mention Sweeney's praise of trees, in particular, as a stirring example of that early nature poetry. Still, even when Sweeney is bemoaning his hardships, his connection to nature in the verse is so immediate, so thoroughly felt, that it strikes the reader as absolutely honest:

All night there I glean and raid
and forage in the oak wood.
My hands feel out leaf and rind,
roots, windfalls on the ground,

they comb through matted watercress
and grope among the bog-berries,
brooklime, sorrel, damp moss,
wild garlic, raspberries,

apples, hazel-nuts, acorns,
haws of the sharp, jaggy hawthorn,
and blackberries, floating weed,
and the whole store of the oak wood.
(*SA*, 65)

This directness appeals to Heaney, who has spent so much of his life describing natural scenes and landscapes in his poetry, and whose symbolic associations are so frequently drawn from nature. Whether or not such a view is at all accurate, the poem does give Heaney the opportunity to draw on and write within a poetry of immediacy.

Nevertheless, for all its attractions, *Sweeney Astray* does not permit Heaney to discover fully the uses to which the title character may be put in his poetry. In order to develop the possibilities he sees in Sweeney, the poet must write his own Sweeney poetry, and he does so in "Sweeney Redivivus," the third section of *Station Island.* The reader will immediately notice that this Sweeney is not identical to the one of the medieval tale. Rather, Heaney had molded him to his own purposes; in this respect he is one of a number of author-surrogates in contemporary poetry, among them Ted Hughes's Crow and Geoffrey Hill's King Offa. Indeed, Sweeney resembles Offa in several important respects: as a medieval king, he is the presiding spirit of a given locale; plucked out of historical context and dropped into the modern age, he offers a disorienting perspective; his presence affords the author the occasion to view "progress" whimsically; and since he is a dramatic persona, he can betray prejudices or make outrageous statements that the poet might be reluctant to utter in his own voice (this last is probably more an attribute of Offa than of Sweeney).

From "The First Gloss" on, "Sweeney Redivivus" announces its intention to make of its character a representative figure for the poet. Indeed, that initial poem, with its injunction to "Take hold of the shaft of the pen" (*SI,* 97), recalls the initial poem of Heaney's first book, in which he delights in the way the "squat pen rests" in his hand. Here, though, the movement is not toward digging with the pen. Rather, the voice becomes literally marginal, taking its initial step "from a justified line / into the margin." This sense of life on the periphery, of exile to the mainstream, becomes the connection point between author and character. Whereas Italo Calvino's eponymous *Baron in the Trees* remains a central figure in life, dispensing wisdom, entertaining women who risk not only shame but physical injury to sample his sexual prowess, Sweeney remains always outside life's feast.

One of Sweeney's main functions, especially early in the sequence, is that of memory. Like poetry itself, he records the transformations: the deforestation, the tilling of the fields, the raising up of towns and cities, the jealousies and wars. In the title poem he awakens to find the river polluted, probably with human waste, and the land cleared:

> The old trees were nowhere,
> the hedges thin as penwork
> and the whole enclosure
> lost under hard paths and sharp-ridged houses.
> (*SI,* 98)

Even here there is the suggestion of writing in the "hedges thin as penwork," and at the poem's end he finds the people "far too eager to believe" him and his story, "even if it happened to be true." The acknowledgment of the writer's power to sway opinion, to make himself credible, may argue somewhat against his marginal position. Yet as the agent of collective memory, he proves attractive to them precisely because they, busy living the life he watches, have forgotten.

Throughout the sequence Heaney uses his own work as source and referent, confidently drawing comparisons to his character's predicament. "Drifting Off," with its litany of birdlife and its image of Ireland as rookery, recalls section 40 of *Sweeney Astray,* Sweeney's celebration of the trees and birds. "In Illo Tempore" takes as its subject the language itself, turning inward on its own creative process in the way Heaney has done countless times in his career. This time he pushes it even further, ruminating not only on the words themselves, but on their forms: "The verbs / assumed us"; "We lifted our eyes to the nouns." He manages here to get beyond specificity, so that ultimately the subject is not the language but Language. Nevertheless, the poem recalls his ceaseless fascination with the materials of his art. It is "On the Road," however, that brings together the greatest number of self-references, from the road "reeling in," which seems to allude to the "unreeled, unreeled" of "Westering," to the "spirit broke cover," recalling "The Badgers." Neil Corcoran has noted a great many of these self-references in his study of the poem, including these direct borrowings as well as his penchant for the optative mode in phrases such as "I would roost . . . I would migrate . . . I would meditate," a pattern from the period of the bog poems.[7] Other characteristics of his earlier verse are evident: the short-line quatrains themselves, the almost incantatory diction, hyphenated compounds and ersatz kennings of a stanza like

> on down the soft-nubbed,
> clay-floored passage,
> face-brush, wing-flap,
> to the deepest chamber.
> (*SI,* 121)

The end-stopped line and caesura in the third line bring the flow of the verse to a nearly complete standstill, showcasing each phrase. This too is the strutting, muscular prosody of *Wintering Out* and *North.* There are also borrowings of types of expression, as in the natural oxymoron of the cutting yet waxy leaves in the delightful "Holly." That poem closes with another typical flourish, picking up the natural metaphor for his artistic activities, when he reaches for a book and wishes it to be "a black-letter bush, a glittering shield-wall / cutting as holly and ice" (*SI,* 115).

All these self-borrowings indicate a writer in full possession of his powers and serenely confident of his art. Yet he is also wiley enough to recognize that such a stance in his own person is a dangerous strategy, and so the Sweeney mask allows him a buffer of sorts. There is no way for the poet to look into Thoor Ballylee at Yeats in his study without the resulting poem seeming too contrived, yet Sweeney, not bounded by the laws of physics, can do it simply. Yeats's idiosyncratic vision notwithstanding, the secret of his poems was "nothing / arcane, just the old rules" (*SI,* 110), yet the result is a measured and solid form—"quarrymen's hammers," "coping stones." His greatness lies in his ability to work within the old rules, and here there is certainly a parallel to Heaney's own approach to poetic form, however inferior he may portray it in the final stanza:

How flimsy I felt climbing down
the unrailed stairs on the wall,
hearing the purpose and venture
in a wingflap above me.

While Yeats is the acknowledged master, there is also kinship here: both are birdmen, and there are "purpose and venture" in Heaney's own wingflappings. Indeed, Heaney's steadfast refusal over the years to go to school to Yeats—this poem's open admiration notwithstanding—testifies to the strength and autonomy of his own vision and poetics.

This sequence, then, stands as a summation of sorts for that individuality, almost a retrospective of certain aspects of his career. A retrospective implies finality, and in "On the Road" he raises the issue, referring to "a dried up source." Perhaps the time to move on inevitably comes at the end of one's books, yet he concerns himself with the problem more explicitly here even than in "Westering" or "Exposure," poems that in their own way foretell changes to come:

For my book of changes
I would meditate
that stone-faced vigil

until the long dumbfounded
spirit broke cover
to raise a dust
in the font of exhaustion.
(*SI*, 121)

These lines presage a phoenixlike rise into a new poetry out of the dust, if not the ashes, of the old Heaney. It may be that he has mined certain veins for all their ore; he has doubtlessly produced much that is golden during the past two decades. If so, he has chosen quite a rhetorical flourish with which to cap a portion of his career. The last lines not only play off the multiple meanings of "font" as baptismal basin, source of plenty, fountain, and set of type, but they also work at least two brilliant oxymorons built off that same word. Heaney has set for himself a large task with his next book, but he has never been one to shrink from daring undertakings.

Chapter Seven

Confronting the Ghosts: *Station Island*

In *Station Island* (1984), appearing six years after *Field Work,* Heaney moves in three different directions. In the first section, he focuses his attention on the world of objects, both man-made and natural. In the second, the title sequence, he follows Dante's example and enters purgatory to encounter his personal, social, and literary history. In the third he offers the series of poems "voiced" as he puts it for mad Sweeney discussed in the previous chapter. Throughout the volume he displays the mastery and assuredness of a mature, accomplished poet, while following interests and preoccupations he has developed through the course of his earlier work.

At first glance, the initial section seems to be a retreat into a objectivist poetry. The titles, "Sandstone Keepsake," "Widgeon," "A Bat on the Road," "Sweetpea," and the individual titles in the small sequence "Shelf Life," all suggest a concentration on things. Yet Heaney is never satisfied merely with objects, with the focus of a miniaturist; he sees something else occurring, some other significance, lurking behind his ostensible subject. His opening poem, for instance, "The Underground" (*SI,* 13), develops a relationship in terms of a pair of walks through the Underground in London. That location seems to suggest another, classical underground, and Heaney draws on classical, folk, and biblical sources. In the opening stanzas the couple is young, and the speaker, a man, pursues the woman "like a fleet god gaining / Upon you before you turned to a reed," a simile drawn from Ovid, as the woman flees, dropping buttons from her topcoat as she goes. The occasion or occasions, we are told in stanza 3, may be any of the events of youth, "Honeymooning, moonlighting, late for the Proms." Time passes, however, "Our echoes die in that corridor," and when they return, the roles are reversed. First, he is Hansel, following the trail of buttons, leading the way:

> To end up in a draughty lamplit station
> After the trains have gone, the wet track

Bared and tensed as I am, all attention
For your step following and damned if I look back.

In this closing stanza he moves from the Brothers Grimm to the Bible to become Lot, not about to become a pillar of salt. These three models share in their portrayal of uneasy or uncertain male power; in each case the male initiates the action, but he cannot be certain of the female's response. Ovid's gods are invariably thwarted by the metamorphoses of their quarry; Hansel in various versions of the tale has problems with the trail he has left and with Gretel; Lot's wife does look back and is lost. Curiously, despite his protestations, the speaker does look back, and the poem develops its power precisely because of the tension between the present and the remembered past.

If the first poem shows Heaney in his serious vein, the second, "La Toilette," offers a more playful look. Like the one before, this poem plays off the present against both the past and cultural forms, in this case liturgical:

The white towelling bathrobe
ungirdled, the hair still wet,
first coldness of the underbreast
like a ciborium in the palm.

Our bodies are the temples
of the Holy Ghost. Remember?
And the little, fitted, deep-slit drapes
on and off the holy vessels

regularly? And the chasuble
so deftly hoisted? But vest yourself
in the word you taught me
and the stuff I love: slub silk.
(*SI*, 14)

I quote in full both because the poem is short and because it proves nearly impossible to discuss sight unseen. The first stanza proceeds normally enough in fairly conventional, mildly erotic language, until the "ciborium" of the fourth line. The ciborium is the vessel for the wafers—for Christ's body—in the communion. In this single word, the poet has made the leap from the erotic to the holy, from a lover's body to the sacred Body.

Nor does he stop there. Recalling the church's stern warning to every child, he tinkers with the analogy between the body and the temple of the Holy Ghost, pushing it in a direction unforeseen in Sunday School or catechism. The act of undressing for lovemaking, then, finds its analog in pulling back the curtain from around the "holy vessels," of lifting the chasuble. But the most delightful maneuver the poem takes is back from the church, from the "vest yourself" of the last sentence, to the purely secular "slub silk." Even here Heaney shows himself a reveller in words, for it is to the "word you taught me" that he first refers in asking her to wear the silk. The tension between the erotic and the liturgical is scarcely original, yet he employs it with such lightness, playing off words in unexpected ways, that it works wonderfully.

That delight in language, in the music of what he's making, is picked up several times through the poems of part 1, notably in "Widgeon," where a hunter picks up the voice box "like a flute stop" from a badly shot up duck he is cleaning. The simile hangs lifeless, even forced, in the poem until he blows through it "unexpectedly / his own small widgeon cries" (*SI,* 48), when suddenly it finds a concrete action to invigorate it. Heaney returns here to one of his common themes, recognizing the importance of making one's own music from what one finds at hand.

Perhaps nowhere in the volume is that insistence clearer than in the sequence, "Shelf Life" (*SI,* 21–24). Comprised of six small poems on objects natural and man-made—"Granite Chip," "Old Smoothing Iron," "Old Pewter," "Iron Spike," "Stone from Delphi," and "A Snowshoe"—the sequence celebrates the lasting power of things and, like so much of his earlier poetry, investigates objects as repositories of racial memory. The granite chip, for instance, is not merely selected at random but knocked from Joyce's Martello Tower, site of the opening scene of *Ulysses.* It is, the poet says, a highly foreign object, cutting his soft hand with its hard, sharp edge, "A Calvin edge in my complaisant pith." The religious intrusion also carries with it geographic overtones—"Aberdeen of the mind," he calls the stone in line 1—and contrasts both with his own falling away from the Church and with the "soft," southern nature of Catholicism. The North is typically represented in his verse by hard sounds, hard surfaces, sharp edges, and here the addition of Calvinism reminds the reader that the northern faith, as practiced, say, by Ulster Protestants, is also hard and sharp. This surprising insertion stems from the surprising qualities he finds in the stone, which is not only "jaggy, salty," but also "punitive / and exacting":

Come to me, it says
all you who labor and are burdened, I
will not refresh you. And it adds, *Seize*
the day. And *You can take me or leave me.*
(*SI,* 21)

It is just this uncompromising quality that fascinates Heaney, even though, or perhaps just because, it wounds him. He finds he has "little in common with" the chip but holds onto it anyway. The poem is remarkable for once again demonstrating the poet's ability to see the world—at least his part of it—in, if not a grain of sand, a chip of stone.

The smoothing iron of the second poem is similarly unforgiving and demanding. In this case the object makes specific demands. It performs no tasks itself, but instead requires the labor of Heaney's mother as a wood-plane (he makes the comparison overt) requires labor of the carpenter. The iron is merely an object, a "compact wedge" that sits on the stove "like a tug at anchor." In using it, his mother forces Heaney to reflect upon the nature of that labor:

To work, her dumb lunge says,
is to move a certain mass
through a certain distance,
is to pull your weight and feel
exact and equal to it.
Feel dragged upon. And bouyant.
(*SI,* 22)

The textbook language is enriched by the reality that invokes it, by "her dumb lunge," "Her dimpled angled elbow / and intent stoop," while the tension between the language of the observer and the silence of the observed worker reminds us, as do so many of Heaney's poems, of the distance as well as the sympathy between the two. In this instance the distance is temporal as well as social or psychological; the action of the poem is entirely a product of memory as he recalls watching her iron in the kitchen. The swimming imagery of the final stanza harkens back to the tugboat of the first and to the description of his mother as she seems to dive into her work with her bent elbow and her angling forward.

In picking up the earlier suggestion for its closing image, this poem points to the individuality of the poems in the sequence. Each poem operates on its own logic, imagery, and prosody, as if each subject demands its own treatment. The pentameter quatrains of the first poem, loosely rhymed *a b a b,* give way in this one to unrhymed trimeter quatrains, and to quatrains in the third, "Old Pewter," again loosely rhymed like the first but with greater variety in line length and scansion. Old pewter, "my soft option" among metals, may suggest to Heaney a similar soft option in his versification—unshowy, homey, undercutting or taking the shine off the rhymes in its conversational rhythm and tone. Old pewter also suggests its own dominant imagery, this time of winter, in its flatness and grayness.

"Iron Spike" finds its imagery in nineteenth-century technology, particularly horse-powered conveyances and the railway from which the spike came. Here again the object pushes Heaney's memory, in this case toward things beyond personal memory to racial or cultural memory. Although the railroad has disappeared, it has left its trace, the spike, that bears witness not only to the rails and ties but also to the sledgehammer that drove it in. Its impact on memory expands to encompass not only the particular situation in which it was used, but the whole milieu of steam locomotion, so that Heaney, wondering what became of the hammer, may say: "Ask the ones on the buggy, / inaudible and upright / and sped along without shadows" (*SI,* 24). The spike then, becomes a key to an unseen world to which the poet does not normally have access—a world that, being "inaudible," does not answer his questions, that casts no shadow. Of course, there is minor irony in the last line, for that other time has cast shadows on our own day, has left traces both in the form of iron spikes and of cultural memories, words, stories, so that the poet can write his poem.

The final poem shares these concerns, yet it handles them in the opposite manner. "A Snowshoe" is in part about writing poetry, yet the act of writing is a principal focus, so that when poetic concerns are raised, they stand as a central, not a tangential, matter. The poet finds the snowshoe when he goes up to the attic "to follow the snow goose of a word." The snowshoe, then, becomes his writing talisman, the sign under which he sits, "a hieroglyph for all the realms of whisper." It also brings with it its own imagery. Just as the railroad spike suggests the creaking harness and the invisible buggy, so the snowshoe brings with it a host of winter images. The room where he envisions it hanging is "drift-still"; the lovemaking that precedes its discovery is an "amorous blizzard." He recalls climbing the stairs like a sleepwalker "scuffling the snow-crust."

The snowshoe, however, also issues in a second, more subtle set of associations. Like the other objects in the six poems, the snowshoe hangs here in a context removed from its original function, which exists merely as a trace, a cultural memory. Moreover, it is not actually present: it exists in the poem only in Heaney's memory. Throughout the poem, then, the poet emphasizes absences, silences. The word he seeks is elusive, a "snow goose," while the snowshoe stands for the "realms of whisper." Sitting in silence, he imagines sounds "like love sounds after long abstinence." In the final stanza he compares the remembered but absent object to "an old-time kite," which "lifts away in a wind and is lost to sight." The sequence celebrates the staying power of objects, certainly, yet it also celebrates the power of poetry to enshrine objects, to capture all-but-lost points of time, for it is finally not in their own right that these stones and implements find their significance but in the responses they evoke from the poet.

The poem preceding "Shelf Life," "Sandstone Keepsake," shares many of the same interests. Indeed, it brings together an astonishing number of his recurring preoccupations around this simple rock. Ostensibly, the poem is about Heaney's finding a piece of sandstone while wading on a beach. Yet as so often happens in his verse, ripeness is all; this particular beach is at Inishowen Head, in County Donegal, across Lough Foyle from the internment camp at Magilligan. The situation lends itself immediately to having recourse to Dante. In the third stanza Heaney imagines the red stone as coming from Phlegethon, the river of boiling blood in the *Inferno.* Moreover, the specific image he employs comes from canto 12, which deals with those who were violent against their neighbors, reminding us of both those interned at Magilligan and those who keep them there. Stanza 4 sees the stone transformed into the heart of the nephew of Henry III, killed in vengeance by Guy de Montfort in the church at Viterbo; the younger Henry's heart was believed to be kept in a casket in London. This allusion is strong stuff, and Heaney cannot maintain it, conceding that it is "not really" as if he held that murdered heart.

Rather, his mind returns to the situation at hand, wading through the lough's waters in "my free state of image and allusion" (*SI,* 20). This clever reference to his location in Donegal, part of the Republic, the Free State, also suggests the freedom accorded the poet in drawing from the world of literature. Yet with that freedom goes a certain lack of power or danger, as he is swooped on, then dropped by trained binoculars:

a silhouette not worth bothering about,
out for the evening in scarf and waders
and not about to set times wrong or right,
stooping along, one of the venerators.

The reference in the penultimate line to Hamlet, who is forced to "set right" the times that are "out of joint," illustrates not only the marginal status of the poet, which he has demonstrated frequently, but his willing resignation to that status. This poem relinquishes the lamenting tone of, for instance, "Exposure," in which he has missed the "once in lifetime portent."

This poem finds him in that same attitude of bending down to the earth, but it connects him with a longer tradition, that of the Irish peasantry. Throughout his poetry Heaney produces images of the people of rural Ireland bending down to earth in work and "homage to the famine god," as he says in "At a Potato Digging." If "stooping along" comprises a major part of Irish work life and religious practice, as he shows from "Digging" to "Station Island," and a political survival for Ulster Catholics, then here it finally also assumes a role in recreation as well.

Part 1 of the book also tries to penetrate the mystery of poetic creativity, without notable success. "The Birthplace," about Thomas Hardy, fails to invoke Hardy on any meaningful level. As Barbara Hardy notes, Heaney's eroticism, in a poem like "Station Island VI," shares with Hardy a delight in "details of dress and flesh."[1] There is something, too, of Hardy's terseness, precision, use of nature, and irony, so perhaps it is logical that he should undertake such a poem (although the Hardy of the poem is the novelist rather than the poet). The descriptions of Hardy's house remain simply that, descriptions; they never find their raison d'être. Moreover, they are frequently strained in the attempt to make them resonate: the single bed is "a dream of discipline," the wind "as slow as a cart / coming late from market" (*SI,* 34). Section 3 of the poem offers a disorienting question: "Everywhere being nowhere, who can prove one place more than another?" (*SI,* 35). In response, he finds himself upon his return home ruminating on the very words that signify home. Yet he drops this comparatively fruitful line of thought for the more artificial discussion of reading Hardy's *Return of the Native.* Only in the middle section, in which he recounts a wounded and driven sexual encounter, does the poem ever come alive, and that occurs because it oversteps its intellectual limits to explore something personal and felt. The failure of this poem, as with so many of Heaney's artist poems, lies in its stiff self-consciousness, its air of needing to be written to fulfill a commitment.

More successful are the volume's several poems that examine the lives of ordinary people around him. "A Migration" moves between the exterior facts of a neighbor girl's return home to live with her mother and younger sisters and an imaginative entry into her inner life. The dream he envisions for her is one of troubled sexuality and maternal demands. Heaney has observed that we live in a society whose myths are Freudian, and the images here—the continuously weeping child, the ship's lounge with empty bottles rolling "at every slow plunge / and lift," and the black taxi pulling into a bombed-out station—read like a litany of Freudian fear and desire. At the same time, Brigid, the girl, offers the poet a vision of responsibility as she shepherds her sisters to fetch water twice daily. Her status as child-woman, replete with growth and anxiety, clearly fascinates the poet. Indeed, while he imagines their trips as incursions against his poetrymaking, he finds, as this poem clearly testifies, the stuff of poetry in them, in her. "The deer of poetry" stand "in our lyric wood" always wary, "ready to scare" as Brigid and her brood come "jangling along," but it is the jangling itself that is the stuff of poetry. Heaney is sufficiently canny to recognize that his forte does not lie in the classical pastoral, that he is a poet of the human scene, and that Brigid is one of his great subjects.

He closes with a long account of a trip—whether real or imagined by him he never reveals—on which Brigid and her sisters miss the bus home to Wicklow. His description of their night journey, as they leave civilization's comfort behind them (even the battery in their cassette player gives out), captures the experience itself while making them refugees of sorts:

> walking south through the land
> past neon garages,
> night lights haloed on blinds,
> padlocked entries, bridges
> swelling over a kind
> mutter of streams.
>
> (*SI,* 27)

The images are all of the human world being closed to them, while the natural world, culminating in "Wicklow's mountainy / black skyline," is wide open. It is in this situation, with the rain beginning, that the poem's closing envisions Brigid taking control. The imagery of the ending, of Brigid's assuming the status of womanhood, with its mountains and swelling streams, its padlocked doors and muttering streams, proves as Freudian as the dream had been. Poet and character are caught up in the same human dimension, and it is that common bond, that level of shared experience or feeling, that makes this poem succeed, makes it touch the reader, while "The Birthplace" remains a distant failure.

Even more personal is his involvement in "An Ulster Twilight," which is about, in some small measure, a very young Seamus Heaney's discovery, one Christmas Eve, that Santa Claus can come in the form of the woodworker down the road. Still, the poem refuses to be satisfied with that moment, which is scarcely more than a beginning. This particular craftsman, Eric Dawson, is Protestant, the son of a constable. There are identifying emblems about him: his father's "uniform and gun," the Raleigh bicycle (an insignia made much of in "Kernes" from *Stations*) on which he makes his delivery run, and a reticence on both sides to say too much or be too open. Even his tools suggest difference to the poet, who envisions "the cold steel monkey-wrench / In my soft hand." All of these we have seen before. Yet their importance for the poem is that they are not important. This man's work and life mark him as part of the same community as the Heaneys, for whom he has built the wooden battleship. In the fourth line he "stoops to his plane," the verb connecting him with the poet's mother, who stoops to her ironing in "Shelf Life," and Heaney himself, stooping along through the surf in "Sandstone Keepsake." His attentiveness to the well-made object, moreover, endears him to the craftsman of the well-made poem, who imagines Dawson working that night

> At five o'clock on a Christmas Eve.
> Carpenter's pencil next, the spoke-shave,
> Fretsaw, auger, rasp and awl,
> A rub with a rag of linseed oil.
>
> (*SI,* 38)

The loving attention Heaney lavishes on listing the objects and sights and smells of the workshop in this poem reveals his admiration for the work done there. Even so, he knows that if the two ever meet again "In an Ulster twilight we would begin / And end whatever we might say / In a speech all toys and carpentry." The Northern Irish reticence, which Heaney has explored frequently, is exacerbated here by differences in professions, educational attainment, religion, and probably politics.

While recognizing those disparities, however, the poet suggests in his last line that maybe not speaking of them was beneficial, that their relationship was "Maybe none the worse for that." The poem acknowledges a profound desire on the part of neighbors to get along, to be neighborly, even in a trying situation. Clearly neither of them made the situation: Dawson's father is the authority figure, and Heaney is only a child. The reference to Yeats's Celtic twilight, moreover, with its dream of a resurrected, united Ireland, implies a desire for wholeness within the divided state of the North. Their silence, the poem suggests, would be an affirmation that the desire is mutually held. The tragedy, as he has shown us in *North,* in *Field Work,* and in the title sequence to this volume, is that such a dream should remain so far out of reach for so long.

Beyond these concerns, of course, the book is also about that most interesting of characters, the poet himself—not only this poet as individual but the activity of poetry. Certainly "Widgeon" points in that direction, as do elements of a number of the short lyrics in part 1. And naturally, both "Station Island" and "Sweeney Redivivus" concern themselves with the poet's role in the world. The poems that close the book's first part, however, may present the most concentrated study of the poetic consciousness in the volume. "The Sandpit," with its parody of *The Waste Land,* clearly intends to be taken as a poem about poetry, and like so many such poems in Heaney's work, draws comparisons to skilled crafts, in this case brickmaking and bricklaying. "The Loaning" examines the writer's involvement with words and images, but especially "lost words," ghostly presences he compares to birds. A loaning, the fallow ground around the edges of a cultivated field, offers a particularly attractive metaphor for Heaney's own poetic method. In his verse the archaic and the arcane vie for our attention, pulling us out of the ordinary, working in "the limbo of lost words" (*SI,* 51). In this sense his poetry very accurately reflects Geoffrey Hill's ideas in his essay "Redeeming the Time," where he asserts that poetry's function is to fight against "the inertial drag of the language." At the same time, however, Heaney's fight against inertia employs the past; his is a language of one's "shades," the ancestral vocabulary that has slipped away. Even his use of the birds as corollaries for words in this poem reminds the reader that his choice for a poetic alter-ego is Sweeney, the ancient birdman.

In the last poem of part 1, then, he invokes Sweeney, or his attempt to know Sweeney, directly. The relationship between poet and character here differs significantly from that with other characters: Heaney has come to know Sweeney not through the purely creative act but through translation. Moreover, as a figure of legend, half-bird and half-man, he is alien to the common run of experience. These two features combine in the poem to unsettle the poet's certainty about his undertaking and to remind him that art is an excursion into the unknown. Sweeney, in the original at home everywhere in Ireland yet without a home, here is a "denless mover," and the poem compares him to "a trespasser" who, opening a unused gate "has opened a dark morse / along the bank." The phrase, recalling the Catholic minority "whispering morse" in "Whatever You Say Say Nothing," suggests the exclusivity of the knowledge of the code. And while Heaney has access to this code, he never quite manages a full look at his subject, remaining instead "haunted" "by his stealthy rustling, / the unexpected spoor, / the pollen settling" (*SI,* 56). Like a hunter stalking his quarry, the poet knows Sweeney only by the sign he leaves. Yet the partnership with the alien works in two directions; if Heaney wishes to know his subject more intimately, Sweeney for his part has depended "on me as I hung out on the limb of a translated phrase." In identifying himself as the haunted, fugitive figure, the poet prepares the way for his entry into the demiworld of "Station Island."

"Station Island"

After mad Sweeney's purgatory in the trees, it is perhaps only fitting that Heaney undergo a purgatory of his own. Throughout his career he has shown a tendency to be haunted by ghosts—familiar, political, literary—and the title sequence in *Station Island* gives the poet the opportunity to confront his ghosts. The occasion for this remarkable experience is a trip to St. Patrick's Purgatory, also known as Station Island, in Lough Derg, County Donegal. The island has been for hundreds of years the destination of pilgrims who follow a three-day ritual of fasting, penance, and worship. Following his custom, Heaney seizes on the ritual as a local, familiar analog to a more exalted and literary example, in Dante, of the situation he seeks to dramatize.

The poet has acknowledged that Dante has occupied much of his reading and thinking over the past several years, and indeed, as far back as *Field Work* (1978) he published a translation of the "Ugolino" section of the *Inferno.* "Station Island" marks an advance of sorts in his relationship to Dante, in that Heaney seeks not so much to borrow, translate, or copy as to employ the *Divine Comedy* as a formal device. His sequence plunges him into the world of the dead, deeper and deeper as it progresses, until he reaches its darkest reaches to encounter a terrorist, and then leads him back out to the world of the living. In this sense he has internalized, absorbed, and re-created Dante in his own image, much as he has already done with Sweeney or, as Barbara Hardy notes, with P. V. Glob: "What one gets from Heaney's Dante, in the 'Station Island' sequence, as from his Bog people, is a new structure for complex experiences of childhood and adolescent recall, an ironic religious sense, and a deep political unease. The new world is rich in images, bright, witty, tender, and rueful, and in ways that are almost entirely expressive of Heaney, not Dante,"[2] That Heaney's work bears evidence of an ironic religious sense or political unease will come as no surprise to readers of his earlier volumes; quite the contrary, this work ratifies much of the thinking of his earlier verse. The only liability (and this very minor) of the *Divine Comedy* as an analog is that, because it is a more predictable source, it lacks some of the force of surprise and delight that the Bog poems lent to *North.*

The title sequence consists of twelve poems, each detailing an encounter with the spirit of some person Heaney has known either personally or through his reading and whose life or death had some impact on him: a sacreligious woodcutter named, significantly, Sweeney; the nineteenth-century novelist William Carleton; an invalid girl; a young priest who died in the missions; some old teachers; Patrick Kavanagh; a girl he was first in love with; a shopkeeper friend who was killed in the night; a friend who died at thirty-two; a young cousin who was shot; a terrorist who died on a hunger strike in jail; an old priest; James Joyce. Most have some message for Heaney, and those messages, far from being of a piece, are often at odds with one another, just as the advice one receives in everyday life (even if one is not a Northern Irish Catholic poet) is often contradictory. What is consistent among the various voices, however, is the sense of expiation of the poet's guilt or anxiety on their behalf. Like characters in an expressionist drama, they speak as Heaney has expected them to speak, voicing his own concerns and fears;

there are few surprises, since these are, after all, his private hauntings made manifest.

The other significant condition of this sequence is that the poet has come to Station Island as one fallen away from belief, at odds with the true believers, so that he frequently finds himself walking the wrong way upon a path, going down as others are coming up, or finding himself suddenly among a group he has not seen before. His sense of estrangement, of solitude among numbers, is reinforced by many of the ghosts with whom he speaks; they accuse him of duplicity, attack his motives, push him away from the retreat and out toward the world. He does not resist.

In the first poem "a hurry of bell-notes" calls the faithful to their stations on a Sunday morning, broken by the shade of a woodcutter, Simon Sweeney, whom Heaney remembers as a "Sabbath-breaker" in life. Like that other Sweeney, he is a blasphemer exiled among the trees, although in this instance it appears to be by choice. He is also one of the familiar types in Heaney's work by now: the craftsman or laborer with whom the poet identifies and sympathizes. We first see him "with a bow-saw, held / stiffly up like a lyre." That Heaney associates the writer's craft with other crafts has become a commonplace, and he introduces it here both because he believes in the analogy and because he wishes to sound a theme that will run throughout the sequence. One major issue he will examine in the sequence is the poet's relation to his past and his environment, his milieu. Here too is Heaney the unbeliever encountering Sweeney the unbeliever, unrepentent even in death, who has always represented a threat of freedom, of detachment from the multitude, of arrogance even. " 'Through gaps in the bushes, / your First Communion face / would watch me cut timber,' " Sweeney tells him; and later, " 'you sensed my trail there / as if it had been sprayed.' "

Heaney finds himself immediately confronted, then, by the possible polarities: Simon Sweeney, whose parting advice is to "Stay clear of all processions," and those faithful pilgrims whose feet "opened a drugged path / / I was set upon." The first line intimates that Heaney is being dragged on in their wake in spite of himself, while the second, coming as it does after a stanza break, reads both as a continuation of the previous sentence, as the end punctuation indicates, and as a new sentence. These "forced" readings suggest not only that he was set upon the path, but the potential danger of being set upon by his fellow pilgrims. The threat they pose to his individuality is only half-hidden. The language of this dichotomy suggests that the poet's loyalties will be almost entirely with the unbelievers. Sweeney is vivid, clearly drawn, inescapable; the pilgrims, who "straggle," their feet "slushing" through the field, have "half-remembered faces." The poem, in fifteen five-line stanzas of unrhymed trimeter, has a curt, at times clipped, pace. This is the line Heaney mastered in the early seventies with the poems that became *North.* In the next poem, in which he meets William Carleton, he extends the line, varying it from nine to twelve syllables, in twenty-three stanzas of three with a widowed seventieth line at the end. The stanzas are either unrhymed or loosely rhymed *a b a,* with the resulting effect of a conversational, at times even haranguing, tone appropriate to the poem's ghost.

The form of these first two poems points to important features both of the sequence itself and of Heaney's mature poetic. Rather than locking himself into a one-size-fits-all form for the entire twelve poems, he chooses to vary line length and stanzaic pattern to fit the circumstances of each verse. When, for instance, he writes of a childhood love, he does so in three sonnets that work together almost as the three movements of a classical ode. Writing of former schoolmasters, he falls into iambic (or, frequently, trochaic) pentameter blank verse. Four times he flirts with the Dantean stanza. In poem 2, detailing his encounter with William Carleton, he moves back and forth between unrhymed lines and the *terza rima* of the *Divine Comedy.* Poem 4 about the young priest is even more irregular in its use of rhyme. The poems about the shopkeeper and Joyce most closely follow Dante, but even there Heaney insists on very loosely rhymed and even occasionally unrhymed lines. Throughout the sequence, he refuses to be dictated to by the metrical form, instead taking liberties as he pleases, rhyming only occasionally and then often quite obliquely, bumping the rhythm just enough to make it play off against the expected scansion, fitting the metrics to the rhythms of spoken language rather than sacrificing speech to poetic convention. This rather freewheeling approach to more or less traditional metrics is an outgrowth of his work in, once again, the early seventies. As Blake Morrison points out, Heaney is often distinctly uncomfortable working within conventional forms in his early years, frequently sacrificing sense or euphony to formal tyranny.[3] He has made the connection, moreover, throughout his career, between the "Orange drums" of Ulster Protestants (a phrase that recurs in his exchange with Carleton) and the "iambic drums" of English poetic tradition. Seeing himself as an outsider, as one whose native rhythms refuse to accommodate themselves to a tidy iambic line, he has had to accommodate the line to *his* metrical needs, first through the short, hard, alliterative lines of *Wintering Out* and, especially, *North,* and in the more relaxed prosody of his subsequent verse.

What astonishes most, however, about "Station Island" is not the range of technical mastery, dazzling though it is, but the range of emotional and psychological states in whose service Heaney employs that technique. The testiness of his encounter with Carleton, for instance, is followed by a vision not of his aunt who died in childhood but of her emblem, "a toy grotto with seedling mussel shells / and cockles glued in patterns over it." The poem is a revery of remembrance, of holding onto a lost sibling through trinkets and through words. The grotto becomes "a shimmering ark, my house of gold," in a phrase from the litany which also recalls young Stephen Dedalus's revery, tinged with innocence and desire at the same time. The ark, moreover, becomes both the ark of the covenant and a nautical vessel in a poem laden with oceanic imagery, while the texture of the shells, which he compares to bird's eggs, leads to an association of the child herself with a bird and ultimately to the remarkable image of her as "a white bird trapped inside me / beating scared wings when *Health of the Sick* / fluttered its *pray for us* in the litany." His return to the present, occasioned by a cold draft, is even harsher than usual because of the subtlety and tenderness of the revery. Heaney thinks of "walking round / and round a space utterly empty, / utterly a source, like the idea of a sound," and his language suggests the emptiness of his current activity, walking round the stations despite the absence of his own belief. That knowledge leads, in its turn, to the closing image not of ocean but of swamp, where he once found the decaying remains of the family dog. That image, recalling an image from his earlier "Kinship" of a dog walking circles on a mat, stands as a self-accusation of the impurity of his motives, of the bad faith of his gesture of pilgrimage.

His motives are further called into question in the following poem, poem 4, in which he encounters a young priest who died doing missionary work in the rain forest. The poem allows a confrontation of middle age by the ghost, literal as well as figurative, of youth, as the priest questions the poet's motives: " 'But all this you were clear of you walked into / over again. And the god has, as they say, withdrawn. / / What are you doing, going through these motions?' " Heaney, noting that he now is older (both older than his former self and older than this ghost who was then his senior) than he was when the priest went away, says of the priest that he was "doomed to the decent thing." The priest's rejoinder, " 'what are you doing here / but the same thing?,' " calls into question the common nature of the two vocations, so that we are not too astonished by the final image of the younger Heaney following the young priest on his rounds through a dreamscape of 'knee-deep mist."

This is a brilliant poem in its own right, even without the support of the remainder of the sequence. Its imagery is concrete, homely, vivid. The native men are "rat-ribbed"; the young priest "rotted like a pear." Heaney, remembering the priest on his bicycle making his visits, here rediscovers his name, which has gone undisturbed for years "like an old bicycle wheel in a ditch" whose "jungling briars" anticipate the rain forest where the priest has died. The priest mentions the steam of the forest, echoed in the steam rising in the final image. The poem's structural tightness plays against its conversational tone in much the same way the metrical form plays against the metrical liberties: creating expectation that are now thwarted, now fulfilled, maintaining a tension of the sort Robert Frost so often exploits in his verse. Ultimately, the sequence succeeds because the individual poems, like this one, work so beautifully on their own.

A similar unity informs poem 6, his three-sonnet-ode to his first love. Set against the classical imagery of Horace, "Loosen the toga for wine and poetry / *Till Phoebus returning routs the morning star*" (whose citation is to remind us that this *is,* after all, an ode), the imagery here is Irish farmyard pastoral, set against the religious: "Shades of the Sabine farm / On the beds of Saint Patrick's Purgatory." He recalls her in terms of "Catkin pixie, little fern-swish." Later, he finds sexual imagery in "bags of grain / And the sloped shafts of forks and hoes . . . Haunting the granaries of words like *breasts.*" The imagery culminates in the third sonnet:

> As if I knelt for years at a keyhole
> Mad for it, and all that ever opened
> Was the breathed-on grille of a confessional
> Until that night I saw her honey-skinned
> Shoulder-blades and the wheatlands of her back
> Through the wide keyhole of her keyhole dress
> And a window facing the deep south of luck
> Opened and I inhaled the land of kindness.

The keyhole recalls the repeated imagery of openings and secrets from the first sonnet, turning into a confessional that plays off that movement's *"Don't tell. Don't tell."* And then the keyhole, in the dress, yields up the most mysterious secret, sex, which again takes a pastoral form in her honey-colored skin and the "wheatlands of her back." Standing as it does as the sixth of the twelve poems, this ode serves as a respite of sorts from the poet's struggle with the larger questions of metaphysics of the previous poems and the politics and violence of the subsequent ones.

Each of the next three poems focuses on a victim of violence, three targets of terrorists and a dead terrorist. Almost immediately in poem 7 Heaney confronts the specter of a murdered shopkeeper, who, responding to a call for help in the night, saw and recognized the two men who bombed his shop. Even in death, he remains an athlete in his prime:

except for the ravaged

forehead and the blood, he was still that same
rangy midfielder in a blue jersey
and starched pants, the one stylist on the team,

the perfect, clean, unthinkable victim.

That last line, again widowed at the beginning of a stanza to call attention to itself, could apply to either of the victims in the following poem, one a thirty-two-year-old archaeologist friend and the other an adolescent cousin. In each case, the victim seemed to have life in front of him, full of promise, at the moment of his death.

They also represent three distinct responses not only to their fates but to the larger Ulster situation. When Heaney attempts to apologize for his lack of direct or passionate involvement, the shopkeeper waves him off, saying "all that's above my head." The cousin, Colum McCartney, offers the other extreme, accusing the poet of complicity through his timid response and his recourse to big abstractions, "live sectarian assassination"; in effect, Colum demands anger, vengeance, retribution. The archaeologist holds out a sort of middle ground, asking Heaney, in his professional capacity, to strive to make sense of events: " 'Ah poet, lucky poet, tell me why / what seemed deserved and promised passed me by?' " It is a question Heaney has encountered before, in "Casualty" from *Field Work,* where the poet imagines himself dared by the murdered fisherman to assign culpability, "Puzzle me /

The right answer to that one." The very rhetoric of the questions suggests their insolubility; theirs is the language of challenge, very much in the manner of Yeats's unknowable questions.

Indeed, the variety of responses Heaney encounters suggests how unenviable his position as poet may be. Where one faction may demand wisdom, insight, or perspective, another, as manifested by Colum McCartney, may demand propaganda, rage, or revenge. To satisfy one is to outrage the other; he cannot mollify all sides, even among these representatives of Catholic Ulster. His dilemma points to the difficulties of his society at large: there are no answers that will satisfy all parties.

After the intensity of these middle poems, the final three offer welcome relief as they ease us, with the poet, back out into the world. The physical movement in poems 8 and 9 is toward night, back to the hostel and to sleep, where in poem 9 Heaney has a strange and troubling dream, and then to morning, where he meets his mirror image with disgust while shaving. We immediately recognize in poem 10 a change of tone, an acknowledgment that this is, after all, a new day:

> Morning stir in the hostel. A pot
> hooked on the forged links. Soot flakes. Plumping water.
> The open door letting in sunlight.
> Hearthsmoke rambling and a thud of earthenware . . .

This is the world not of confrontation and politics and ghosts but of home (if temporary) and hearth. Objects are solid; the scene is made of nouns, and what verbs appear function as participles. This poem also reveals Heaney reverting to linguistic playfulness. The water "plumps," harking us back to the words original German meaning, "to fall into water." The hardness of the line, "A pot / hooked on forged links," helps convince us of the solidity of the pot and the chain, and when the door admits sunlight into the room to filter through the "rambling" smoke, we feel the sense of ease and warmth has permeated the poem as well as the hostel.

The poem continues in this new mood, concerned not with ghosts but with memories and the staying power of things, taking as its focus the appearance of a mug sitting on a high shelf. To that extent it continues some preoccupations from the first section of the volume, particularly as articulated in "Shelf Life." The mug, with its cornflower pattern, provokes memory and personal history as the poet recalls seeing it used as an improbable stage prop in a play, a small miracle in itself, "until the curtain / jerked shut with an ordinary noise." In this morning at the hostel, then, it again occasions, by its mere presence, a sense in the poet of the miraculous, that it has survived against all likelihood, survived submersion in forgetfulness as—and here he makes the comparison overt—Saint Ronan's psalter survived Sweeney's tossing it into the lake. It is this sudden manifestation of the miraculous, like Hopkins's inscape or Joyce's epiphany, that fascinates: "The dazzle of the impossible suddenly / blazed across the threshold, a sun-glare / to put out the small fires of constancy." If the fabric of ordinary life can be rent in an instant by a bullet or a bomb—and the ghosts in these poems testify that it can—then it can also be obscured by the blinding flash of miracle or genius or inspiration, though that inspiration come from the most ordinary of objects. For a poet who shares in the postmodernist obsession with self-awareness in the creative act, surely such a notion has implications for his writing, and indeed, many of Heaney's finest poems have that shock of the ordinary suddenly touched by the impossible. *North* is an entire volume tinged with such a feeling: the discovery of those pictures in Glob's book brought the whole social and political situation into perspective and allowed Heaney to write a poetry far stronger than anything he had previously done.

The poem at hand is the product of such a miraculous moment, as is the next one, poem 11, or at least part of it. In the poem, Heaney reencounters an old priest's ghost and takes literally his advice: " 'Read poems as prayers,' he said, 'and for your penance / translate me something by Juan de la Cruz.' " The imagery here in the first section is of jewels, kaleidoscopes, lightships, particularly as they shine forth out of darkness or muddied water, implying the element of wonder and brilliance of what is to follow. The second part of the poem, then, is a translation from by St. John of the Cross, in which the poet envisions the "eternal fountain" and praises its properties in triplets consisting of rhymed pairs of lines with the third line refrain, "although it is the night." The translation, then, like the framing poem, is concerned with objects shining forth in darkness, with the fountain "So pellucid it never can be muddied," with the gift that is unexpected, undeserved, out of all proportion to merit. It becomes for Heaney the thing it describes, the poem-as-prayer, and it provides him with the chance, mentioned by the old monk, "to re-envisage / the zenith and glimpsed jewels of any gift / mistakenly abased," despite attesting to a belief in which Heaney does not share.

Taken together, these two poems provide Heaney with, if not *Paradiso,* a way out of purgatory, a sustaining vision of the poet's role. If he cannot, with St. John of the Cross, drink at the fountain of religious faith, he can at least embrace his craft as the making of things that give meaning, that have value, that last. This stance may be a retreat of sorts from the challenges to his writing and what it can accomplish in poems 7 through 9, yet it is also liberating. For fifteen years circumstances have forced him to contend with political events. How salutary, then, to be reminded that poetry has functions other adjudicating partisan squabbles or raising the tribal banner. Comforting too, even for an unbeliever, is the notion that there may be some matters beside which even the apparently insurmountable Troubles may seem dwarfed, that light exists somewhere, "although it is the night."

Having come through St. Patrick's Purgatory and arrived at this point in his experience and thinking, Heaney is nearly ready to rejoin the world again. There remains but one more shade to encounter, at once the most literary and most worldly of all the ghosts he meets, one of the two figures (the Catholic one) with which an Irish writer must strive. Even before we see the figure, we can be fairly sure from the "fish-cold and bony hand" that it is Joyce. Here again, Heaney works in a playful mood, bending Joyce's language back against him, the tall, straight, seemingly blind man walking with Stephen Dedalus's ash plant, a voice "eddying with the vowels of all rivers" from *Finnegans Wake.* Heaney addresses him as "Old father, mother's son," in a direct parody of Stephen's address to his namesake in the *Portrait.*

If Joyce's appearance is nearly inevitable, it has also caused the most trouble for readers and critics. Like the other ghosts, Joyce has a very definite point of view regarding the poet:

> 'Take off from here. And don't be so earnest,
>
> let others wear the sackcloth and ashes.
> Let go, let fly, forget.
> You've listened long enough. Now strike your note.'
> (*SI,* 93)

A number of critics have found the three literary appearances, and Joyce's in particular, forced or jarring. Robert B. Shaw, for instance, finds little that's believable in Joyce's advice, "the speech seems not only flat, but for Heaney, *wrong.* What have we been listening to throughout the sequence if not to his 'note' at its most sonorous?"[4] Yet others, such as Nicholas Christopher, find the encounter with the master the high point of the sequence.[5] The key, I believe, lies in Joyce's comments, which are at once delightfully Joycean and exasperatingly wrongheaded, which may mean they are more typical than contradictory.

This is Joyce the elitist. " 'Your obligation / is not discharged by any common rite' " (*SI,* 92), he says, and later, " 'Keep at a tangent. / When they make the circle wide, it's time to swim / out on your own . . . ' " (*SI,* 93–94). This advice may be antidotal for a poet so often pulled by the strings of community loyalty, yet it sounds like better advice for Joyce than for Heaney. Moreover, his insistence on forgetting, on being less earnest, on leaving the English language to the dead does not even sound like advice for Joyce. It echoes language Stephen might use, particularly in his diary entries, but it does not represent a course Joyce himself followed. Perhaps we are mistaken to expect his advice to be any more valuable than any of the others in "Station Island." His is, after all, only one voice among many, and the fact that it appears last may not make it the final word, however much it may appear that way. Still, he sounds a criticism of Heaney's current activity that may ring true for the reader. "That subject people stuff is a cod's game," he says, "infantile, like your peasant pilgrimage" (*SI,* 93). Heaney may be going through the motions of the pilgrimage, Joyce reminds us here, but not under the same terms as the other pilgrims. This is not an act of atonement; rather, it is the occasion to gather literary materials. Joyce, then, provides Heaney with the device he needs to undercut those who, like himself, may be inclined to take his enterprise too seriously. Literature is play, after all, and the playfulness of Heaney's language here as elsewhere in the sequence suggests he does not really need that advice.

Whether or not one approves altogether of Heaney's use of Joyce in the poem, his parting comments and disappearance make up for any minor stumbling. Telling Heaney to swim out on his own, Joyce says to "fill the element"

> 'with signatures on your own frequency,
> echo soundings, searches, probes, allurements,

> elver-gleams in the dark of the whole sea.'
> The shower broke in a cloudburst, the tarmac
> fumed and sizzled. As he moved off quickly
>
> the downpour loosed its screens round his straight walk.
> (*SI,* 94)

Again Heaney presents us with the mix of hard fact, even scientific data, in the "echo soundings, searches, probes," and the marvelous, in the "elver-gleams," pointing as they do not only to the flash of immature eels but also to the elves lurking within the word. That curious mixture also informs the elder writer's exit. Each appearance and disappearance in the sequence has occasioned a kind of wonder, and Joyce's departure, in the very last line, has about it an element of marvel that movie endings once had: the tall, erect figure suddenly obliterated by the natural world, by the sunset or, as in this case, the downpour. The supernatural world in which the poet has moved during the sequence yields to the natural; the revelatory gives way to the mundane.

Heaney refuses to frame the sequence by letting us see him back out in that world, nor does he need do so. The structure of the experience allows him simultaneously to participate directly in the action, in the encounters, and to step back to offer some kind of perspective on events. Always the postmodernist, he approaches his material warily, at once using and mistrusting it, offering a self-portrait that Helen Vendler, writing in the *New Yorker,* calls a mix of "Chaucerian irony and Dantesque earnestness."[6] He listens to Colum McCartney's accusations but does not give in to them; he loathes himself in the morning mirror but recognizes the posturing implicit there; he presents Joyce's purism but shows us no result. Or rather, it is all result: this poem is the product not only of a trip through purgatory, but also (and we must remember it is in the past tense throughout) of resurfacing, of rejoining the world in order to write it.

Chapter Eight

Facing Life, Facing Death: *The Haw Lantern*

In his seventh volume of original poetry, Heaney returns to many of his recurrent preoccupations: his agricultural beginnings, familial relationships, political realities in Ulster, conflicting demands made by the forces of society, the seeking of truth, the literary and linguistic connection to other northern nations, love of the sound and etymology of words. Yet readers coming to *The Haw Lantern* (1987) from the earlier books will be struck by the formal novelty of these poems. Consistent with his refusal to stay in the same place poetically, to write the same book more than once, Heaney breaks new ground in his most recent volume. The two most striking features of *The Haw Lantern* are the highly personal, even confessional, sonnet sequence on the death of his mother and the frequent essays into allegorical and parable poetry scattered throughout the volume. These new developments point to a personal poetic that is robust, dynamic, and resolutely forward-looking in a career whose success might tempt a poet to try to repeat past accomplishments.

There are a number of discernible influences leading to the newer poetic style. One, of course, is the continuing impact of Dante. In *Field Work* he borrows imagery and phrasings from the *Divine Comedy;* in the title sequence from *Station Island* he borrows the device of the poet's journey out of life. Here the influence is less immediate. Dante's trilogy is nothing if not an extended parable, a cautionary tale; without encroaching on the specifics of form, Heaney emulates Dante in turning his poetry to particular instructional purposes. Another source of change, only partly literary, arises from the occasions for which Heaney wrote certain of these poems, particularly "From the Republic of Conscience," written for the Amnesty International Irish Section's 1985 Human Rights Day observance, and "Parable Island," written for William Golding and published in a festschrift celebrating that writer's seventy-fifth birthday. Golding stands as England's premier allegorist since Orwell, and Heaney's approach in this poem as well as others seems to reflect an admiration for the novelist's relation to his art. The fable, the allegory, the parable represent another option to an exasperating situation other than despair and withdrawal on the one hand, or rage, didacticism, and satire on the other.

Yet another influence for change in Heaney's poetry is his experience in America while teaching at Harvard over the last several years. That influence, as he explains, however, is neither that of contact with American writers nor of American subject matter, but something much more tenuous and ephemeral, something that ties in with the distance he has maintained ever since *Wintering Out* from his first world:

> I don't know what the gains are, or what the losses are. All I know is it would have felt to me like exploitation of a patented subject and connivance with a slightly folksified reputation if I had kept on writing of County Derry and the days of the churn. Your literary innocence evaporates, and if it doesn't it should. As Eliot says, we hope to write the poems that are appropriate to the stage of life that we're at.

This recognition of the need for distance has led him physically to the Irish Republic, to Spain and to the United States, and imaginatively from the Vikings to Dante to Joyce, yet the foot of the compass has remained always in that world of his early experience, so that no matter how far his wanderings might seem to take him, Heaney's work is always tethered to Ulster, as if the shadow-man he might have been had he remained at home demanded recognition. *The Haw Lantern,* then, follows that pattern, for its poems continue to originate from a consciousness very much identifiable in terms of place and ethnicity:

> I've not written about being in America, I suppose, partly because of ideological reasons almost. I believe where you live isn't necessarily what you have to write about; the given for your subject or your imagination, isn't necessarily your environment. On the other hand, the distance and the slight permissiveness, the slightly gravitiless life that I have had here has freed me in some ways to be more chancy in writing. In the new book there are a number of poems that are kind of parable poems. There's a poem called "From the Frontier of Writing," which uses an encounter at a roadblock, a kind of archetypal, Ulster, Catholic situation. It turns it into a parable for the inquisition and escape and freedom implicit in a certain kind of lyric poem. You know, you cross the bar and you're free into that other region.
>
> I would say the American experience may have confirmed and assisted what

I think happens anyway as you get toward your fifties, that is a certain rethinking of yourself, a certain distance from your first self.

The physical distance then reinforces the psychological and emotional distance that, while not overturning the validity of the earlier experience or negating the importance of origins, casts the accumulated past in a new frame of reference.

Field Work stands as the first of the mature works that at least borders on being middle-aged. This book goes beyond that to being fully conscious of the writer as situated firmly in middle age. In *The Haw Lantern* the poet's middle age reveals itself in the reminiscences about earlier life, in the attitude toward death not as some horrid surprise but as an inevitable event, and in the overall maturity of voice and vision.

That maturity affords the poet perspective on experience, both the youthful and adult varieties, in a poem such as "Alphabets," which explores his lifelong involvement with written language. The verse moves, as Neil Corcoran notes in his *Times Literary Supplement* review, from letters apprehended and understood in terms of experience, from *Y* as a forked stick or *A* as "Two rafters and a cross-tie on a slate,"[1] to experience apprehended in terms of writing, the "printouts" of balers replacing the older "lambdas" of sheaves in the stubble field.[2] Throughout the poem the movement is from the local and personal toward the universal, until we reach the image of an astronaut viewing the world from his capsule. In an earlier Heaney poem, the progression might have satisfied the poet's need to understand. Here, on the other hand, that movement is countered by certain constants. For instance, the imagery is chiefly agricultural; script writing lies "like briars coiled in ditches"; the poet recalls the time of a scribe "Who drove a team of quills on a white field"; he understands the potato pit as having a "delta face." Heaney remains always a product of his agrarian beginnings, and this poem declares again that allegiance to his first environment.

The world, moreover, remains as much beyond the man as the boy. The image of the globe, that ultimately ungraspable abstraction, recurs in the various sections; that image tends to undercut the smug illusion of personal progress. The man has become a man because "The globe has spun"; he has had no power to control the course of time and event, and if he is able, with the astronaut, to understand that spinning ball as an "aqueous, singular, lucent O," it nevertheless surpasses understanding as much as the magic of the plasterer who, before the poet's "prereflective self," trowelled the family's name above the doorway. That sense of smallness and powerlessness has been present throughout Heaney's career, frequently as alienation from the extremes of political unrest. Here, however, the distance is more metaphysical: both the letters and the dislocation from the world are acts of defamiliarization, of "making strange," to use the term from *Station Island.* Looking at the world as something profoundly Other may, in turn, offer the poet a new perspective, a vantage point from which he may attempt new poems. The placement of "Alphabets" as the initial poem in the book, then, announces the poet's intention to try to see things differently, to take an alternate approach to his subject matter.

Heaney has lived in a time of extremes, yet he has always been able to point out the ordinary within the radical; here, he comes upon the radical in the ordinary. Nowhere is that propensity for finding the unexpected, the allegorical within the quotidian more pronounced than in the first of the parable poems, "From the Frontier of Writing." While the situation out of which the poem grows, being stopped at a military roadblock, is scarcely an everyday occurrence, it is, as he says "an archetypal, Ulster, Catholic situation." Throughout the piece, phrasings pop up that make it clear that this is a repeated action. The "you" of the second person mode of address suggests a familiarity with the scenario. The driver feels "a little spent / as always" by the psychic strain of the interrogation at the first checkpoint. Moreover, there is no alarm or even hint of surprise; the matter-of-fact tone itself indicates the repetition of the action. Even the repeated phrasings from earlier books—"the black current of a tarmac road" from his Joycean encounter in "Station Island" and the "polished windscreen" so prevalent, as Corcoran has noted, in *Wintering Out*—point to the routine nature of the confrontation. Indeed, it is entirely appropriate that the encounter be routine, for Heaney is speaking not of some horrific event the poet must overcome but of the mundane and ordinary subjugation of self from which he escapes when he enters the world of the lyric poem. The "inquisition and escape and freedom" grow out of the commonplace, not the spectacular.

The lyric becomes in this scenario an affirmation of self, of individual autonomy and separateness in a world where self is constantly threatened: the final image is of the driver protected from the menacing soldiers by the windshield of the car, which they have challenged but ultimately not violated. The poem reminds us, at the same time, of how much of Heaney's own work has come about in a time of checkpoints and suspicion, and of how that work stands for affirmation of humanity in the face of inhumane circumstances.

The movement from common experience to allegory informs several of the parable poems, notably "From the Land of the Unspoken" and "Parable Island." The former of these plays off the many earlier poems in which silence and inarticulateness form the core of the action. Often they involve Heaney's father, or the neighboring farmers of his childhood, or those common laborers like the fisherman Louis O'Neill, or the poet himself: people wary of speech, mistrustful of language, conscious of how easily one may say the wrong thing. Indeed, in conversation, although he is a congenial and at times talkative man, Heaney often gives the impression of holding back, of choosing with great care not only his words but which elements of himself he wishes to reveal. He is, after all, the writer of that anthem for the Land of the Unspoken, "Whatever You Say Say Nothing." The poem reminds readers of the curious paradox of a writer who, while on the one hand celebrating language throughout his career, has maintained a lifelong wariness about the damage language can do.

In fact, this poem too recalls images of silence from Heaney's earlier work like the "absolutely silent quernstones" (*N,* 18) of the bog poem period. In *North* the quernstones were silent repositories of history; here, they are the object of pretended consideration by a fellow nonspeaker the poet encounters on the subway. Similarly, the water and fishing imagery that have so often accompanied silent people recurs here both as the "flooding" "solidarity" that citizens of this quiet land feel and as the jumping fish whose ripples announce the deaths of those citizens. These are a very private people, so much so that "the first of us to seek / assent and votes in a rich democracy / will be the last of us and have killed our language." The poem, moreover, threatens constantly to collapse into silence, working as it does against expectations of conventional prosody. While many lines contain ten or even twelve syllables, the line length of pentameter verse, in other words, the heavy use of unstressed syllables, of dactyls and anapests, tends to deflate the rhythm from any pretentions to music that poetry might entertain. Coupled with the blank verse and the frequent feminine line endings, the metrical oddity pushes the verse toward prose, emphasizing the quiet, low-key personality of a citizen of the Land of the Unspoken.

The power of silence and the distrust of speech, of noise, also inform "From the Republic of Conscience." It is a "frugal" land, without porters, interpreters, or taxis, where public officials weep upon inauguration "to atone for their presumption to hold office" and where the visitor carries "your own burden and very soon / your symptoms of creeping privilege" vanish. There is not the usual noise and contentiousness at the airport; when the airplane is shut off, the runway is so quiet the poet can hear a curlew high overhead. The old immigration clerk shows a picture of the poet's grandfather, and upon departure, this same clerk simply looks into the poet's face to confer dual citizenship. Significantly, the old man also requests Heaney to speak for the republic "in my own tongue," an acknowledgment that conscience is essentially mute, that it attains public notice only when those who practice it elect to speak for it. Indeed, throughout the poem there are reminders of the essentially private nature of conscience, which unlike politics, has no program. Public officeholders must vow to obey "unwritten laws." Encounters between officials and visitors or citizens are invariably one on one; it is a land without pomp or mass movements. And so it is with conscience: we obey unwritten rules, conduct activities not because of some outside enforcer but because we know them to be right, carry our own burdens of guilt, weep in atonement for our own crimes. How much influence conscience has in our lives is a matter of our choosing, and we may if we wish speak on its behalf. None of this is earth-shaking, of course, yet it is the imagery with which Heaney constructs his imaginary republic that makes it so convincing. The poem is a lesson not so much in how to behave as in how to build a world, complete with belief system and public institutions. We know, for instance, that these people fear fog and hope for lightning, that salt is their precious mineral, that "Their sacred symbol is a stylized boat. / The sail is an ear, the mast a sloping pen, / The hull a mouth-shape, the keel an open eye" (*HL,* 12). The symbolism of the various elements of the boat is fairly obvious, and indeed perhaps it should be, since it is their boat and not, ostensibly, his. More important is the way it fits into the whole of the creation. In these several allegories Heaney explores a new dimension of what he perceives as the poet's vatic function: seer, sage, emissary of vision and truth.

The final two parable poems, "Parable Island" and "From the Canton of Expectation," play off the reader's knowledge of Heaney's situation as a Northern Irish writer. In the former the initial stanza clearly suggests a very familiar geography and a mindset:

> Although they are an occupied nation
> and their only border is an inland one

> they yield to nobody in their belief
> that the country is an island.
> (*HL,* 10)

The isolationist impulse points to, in the first instance, the competing beliefs of Ulster militant Protestants, who see themselves as an outpost of the British Empire in the midst of a hostile nation, and the militant Catholics, who see themselves as an enclave of Irish Nationalism swamped by colonizing usurpers. The social and political importance the poem attaches to dialectal variation harkens directly back to "The Ministry of Fear" and "Whatever You Say Say Nothing." Even the "fork-tongued natives . . . repeating / prophecies they pretend not to believe" sounds a familiar note, as the first section dredges up old images.

Yet this poem goes determinedly beyond Heaney's earlier work. Not content with recording the Troubles, it insists on universalizing the situation, for this is not Ulster specifically but simply a place like it. In conversation, Heaney compares the situation of the writer in the North of Ireland to writers in the American South, citing specifically Flannery O'Connor and William Faulkner. That he sees parallels to other situations indicates the broad perspective in which he can place the predicament of his homeland:

> If you come from a situation where truth and justice are not generally at work, and you are a product of that contorted place, whether a minority product or a majority product, you have some imperative that comes with your vocation to deal with that. That's a fundamental demand that writers from the North of Ireland face, it's a demand from within themselves, to discover a path into proper thinking, action, and composure.

This comment, made a week before the publication of *The Haw Lantern,* suggests that Heaney is still concerned with the state of affairs in Northern Ireland and also that he sees it in the broader context of human difficulties, for of course Ulster is not the only spot on earth where truth and justice are not generally at work in society. It may be that here his American experience has borne fruit, in affording him a greater distance and a radically different social situation from which to view the Troubles.

Several lesser poems also exploit the new visionary stance: "The Song of the Bullets," "The Disappearing Island," "The Mud Vision," and the title poem. What these pieces share is an attempt to get at truth symbolically and allegorically rather than through realistic description. "The Haw Lantern" stands as the most surprising and rewarding of these. The haw first transforms from fruit to lantern, "a small light for small people" asking only that "they / keep the wick of self-respect from dying out" (*HL,* 7), and then transforms again to the "roaming shape of Diogenes" looking for not an honest man but "one just man." The inquisition-in-miniature seems to suggest itself by the uncompromising nature of the hawthorn, with its "burning" fruit and its "bloodprick" of thorn; the sudden rightness of the association makes "The Haw Lantern" an outstanding example of a poem in the symbolist-imagist tradition that poetry in this century has so often sought after and so seldom achieved. It attains to Pound's "emotional and intellectual complex in an instant of time" in a manner that, like Pound's "In a Station of the Metro," is nearly beyond words: one is surprised into assent.

The poem also illustrates a very clear trend in the volume toward the use of classical figures and myths: not only Diogenes but Socrates in "A Daylight Art," Hermes in "The Stone Verdict," Penelope in "The Stone Grinder," Constantine in "Alphabets." By these references, which often form a poem's conceit, Heaney runs the risk that the resulting poem will become, like "The Stone Grinder," overly self-conscious. The comparison in this poem between the archetypal faithful wife at her loom and the stone grinder fails to convince, seeming contrived, academic in the worst sense. The tale of Socrates translating Aesop on his last day of life, having discovered too late that his true calling was for poetry rather than philosophy, is more satisfying, perhaps because the poem is more open, more humorous. The reader is not asked to take matters quite so seriously, and perhaps for that reason the analogy seems less strained. Certainly the greater use of classical history and myth points in any event to a wider frame of reference in Heaney's work, following a path blazed initially by his interest in Dante during the mid-1970s.

One should not suppose, however, that he has abandoned Irish subjects or treatments altogether in *The Haw Lantern.* "The Old Team" describes a photograph of a turn-of-the-century football team in a generic pose and setting, which in turn becomes the occasion for remembering a kind of lost grace, in which "Team spirit, walled parkland, the linen mill" have "grown historical" (*HL,* 23). Wolfe Tone speaks in an eponymous poem, recalling his misfortune to be "out of his element" among peasant farmers after the break-up of the French fleet. His description of himself as 'manoeuvrable / yet outmanoeuvred" (*HL,* 44) could stand as an image of virtually the entire history of Irish insurrection. "A Shooting Script" offers a treatment for a movie of the death and rather academic rebirth of the Irish language in this century, complete with the very filmic ending of a stick tracing "Words in the old script" in the sand as waves break over and obliterate them. Ireland is obviously always close to Heaney's heart and mind, providing him with some striking short lyrics in this book.

Yet the most completely Irish, Ulster situation of all arises in his remarkable sonnet sequence, "Clearances," written in memory of his mother, who died in 1984. In it, Heaney reimmerses himself in the familial, domestic world he once seemed to have abandoned in his verse. Still, this is not the simple, homely poetry of those first two books; "Clearances" has a distance the earlier poetry lacked and the lean muscle of his more recent work. The fifth of the eight sonnets, about folding sheets with his mother, for instance, bears some resemblance to "Churning Day," although Heaney himself acknowledges some major differences:

> In "Churning Day," that's a young fellow entranced with words and learning to write. "Churning Day" has got too many words in it. It's kind of thick, in love with the idea of writing like Hopkins. In the sonnets, first of all they're sonnets, which is slightly different. They are a dance of sorts. And the folding of the sheets one is about lines rather than textures, lines of force, that's the theme of the thing.

The change is inevitable, dictated by growth and maturity as much as by a need to develop new forms: "A writer cannot dwell completely in origin. Origin is almost Eden, you know. You have to leave Eden and get the division; the loss of Eden, the memory, is one of the ways writing occurs." Still, that "patented subject" of which he speaks earlier remains a part of his existence, and return to it he does. Yet in these memorializing sonnets the tone is exactly one of the loss of Eden, or of his closest tie with the old place.

His description of the sonnets as a kind of dance has particular applicability to the fifth sonnet, for he and his mother are engaged there in a highly ritualized dance, tethered together by a freshly laundered sheet:

> So we'd stretch and fold and end up hand to hand
> For a split second as if nothing had happened
>
> . . . .
>
> In moves where I was x and she was o.
>
> (*HL,* 29)

There is an elegant simplicity to both the action described and the language used to describe it that stands in marked contrast to "Churning Day," where the emphasis is all on thickness and heaviness. Here, the first two lines set the tenor, "The cool that came off sheets just off the line / Made me think the damp must still be in them" with their long run of monosyllables and their absolute regularity of scansion, iambic in the first, trochaic in the second. Even the consonance of the *m* in the second line is understated, gentle. The Hopkinsian Heaney of *Death of a Naturalist* or the Anglo-Saxon Heaney of *North* would have stacked those consonantal chimes on top of each other—and would probably have chosen a harder phoneme in any event. Yet the mature Heaney displays such assuredness in his craft that he no longer feels he must overwhelm the line with evident mastery. These sonnets manifest a further opening of form first displayed in the "Glanmore Sonnets." After fighting for so many years against "the tyranny of the iamb," the poet seems finally not only to have made peace with it, but also to have harnessed it to his own purposes.

The sequence is intensely private, growing out of completely, personal memories. As Margaret Heaney's eldest child, he experienced a great many intimate moments—folding sheets, peeling potatoes while the rest of the family was at mass, even the oedipal struggle of what he calls "our *Sons and Lovers* phase"—that the younger siblings could not share quite so exclusively. Even the point of entry is a symbol of privacy, a cobblestone thrown at his great-grandmother by outraged Protestant neighbors when she married a local Catholic. After envisioning the scene in which the stone was thrown, he goes on in the sestet to identify the real significance: "Anyhow, it is a genre piece / Inherited on my mother's side / And mine to dispose with now she's gone" (*HL,* 25). In this first sonnet he establishes himself as a clear inheritor of the maternal side of his family, both sympathetically and, thanks to the keepsake, materially.

That inheritance expresses itself clearly throughout the sequence. Heaney's father is simply *he,* an outsider admitted into the fold in the seventh sonnet. In the second piece Heaney again enters the maternal side imaginatively, this time envisioning his mother being welcomed to her new home, "Number 5, New Row, Land of the Dead," as she had been welcomed into his home in life. This poem offers a particularly compelling example of sonnet form. The octave recalls dining rituals of his childhood: rules, maxims, practices of a clean, well-ordered kitchen:

> Polished linoleum shone there. Brass taps shone.
> The china cups were very white and big—
> An unchipped set with sugar bowl and jug.
> The kettle whistled.
>
> (*HL*, 26)

With its crisp diction and clipped sentences it brings to mind the tenth poem in the "Station Island" sequence, which is also about domesticity and kitchen life in particular. After a physical break the sestet picks up the scene in the afterlife, presenting a radical disjuncture in theme, tone, and prosody. The final six lines are much more open rhythmically, running through three consecutive lines, 10 through 12, with neither caesura nor endstop. The result of this highly Coleridgean yoking together of discordant elements, aside from startling the reader momentarily, is the poet's being placed firmly in his mother's camp.

The following sonnet, the third, corroborates that situating of loyalties, showing mother and son as co-conspirators who shared chore and silence while the rest of the family was out of the house. It too leaps suddenly to the present in the sestet, affording the poet a chance to show himself remembering this scene while the priest "Went hammer and tongs at the prayers for the dying" (*HL*, 27). That moment of alliance brought them together so that they were "Never closer the whole rest of our lives." Significantly, that closeness occurred on her territory, not his.

The fourth poem, then, establishes the distance the adult Heaney found himself removed from that first world, his mother feigning incompetence in his chosen field, "as if she might betray / The hampered and inadequate by too / Well-adjusted a vocabulary." (*HL*, 28). The sonnet concerns itself with words on the syntactic as well as thematic level, rhyming "affect" with "*Bertold Brek,*" and repeating key words—"inadequate," "well-adjusted," "affectation"—to convey the notion of curbing one's language as a demonstration of filial piety, a practice that a great many people whose educations supersede those of their parents will recognize. With the fifth sonnet presenting a ritual dance of domesticity between mother and son, the sixth completes the cycle of life between them in its depiction of worship. Holy Week services became "highpoints of our *Sons and Lovers* phase" (*HL,* 29), an interpretation that suggests how far he is now removed from that period. The worship they share, kneeling next to each other through ritual described very precisely, forms its own ritual. Like the preceding activities, the apparently un-self-conscious activity reveals itself as a highly self-conscious stylization to memory. The patterns observed form an acceptable, comprehensible way for mother and son to act out the love between them.

Yet for all the insights and the wonderful language use of these first six sonnets, the sequence could not stand without the final two astonishing poems. The seventh sonnet begins by revealing Heaney's father's attempts to provide solace to his dying, unconscious wife, saying more at the end "Almost than in all their life together," (*HL,* 31). The passage reminds us that the elder Heaney has always appeared in the poems as a taciturn, almost tongue-tied farmer whose emblem of silence is the harvest bow. In the midst of his assurances, the octave ends with the simple statement that "Then she was dead," opening the way for the terrifically moving sestet:

> The searching for a pulsebeat was abandoned
> And we all knew one thing by being there.
> The space we stood around had been emptied
> Into us to keep, it penetrated
> Clearances that suddenly stood open
> High cries were felled and a pure change happened.

These six lines may be the most affecting verse he has ever written; certainly it is difficult to imagine anything that could be more so. The apparent artlessness of the prosody—absence of rhyme, prose-imitating irregularity of rhythm, simplicity of diction—contributes to the apparent spontaneity and veracity of the feeling. The mature Heaney has learned what Philip Hobsbaum complained the youthful Heaney failed to understand, that technique is sometimes the suppression of craft. In this instance, restraining mastery makes for poetry of great power.

The final sonnet builds on the image of absence introduced in the sestet, drawing at the same time on an passage already used in "Station Island III," that of "walking round and round a space / Utterly empty, utterly a source" (*SI,* 32). But whereas in the "Station Island" poem the image remains rather abstract, in this poem he finds its objective correlative, a chestnut tree that no longer exists:

My favorite is the last one, which is about the tree which isn't there anymore. I think it's a middle-aged poem. It's as much about me and my state as about my mother's departure. I just had begun to think about the space where this tree had been. It was my birth tree, really, a chestnut tree my Aunt Mary had planted the year I was born at Mossbawn. We left Mossbawn when I was thirteen, fourteen. And the people who moved in after us cut down all the trees around the place, and I never gave a thought to that.

The loss of his mother, however, set him to thinking about this other loss from childhood, of an object by which he could measure and identify himself. The reminiscence he considers particularly middle-aged:

Then recently, I had been thinking about empty spaces. I began thinking about Yeats's play *At the Hawk's Well,* which is about a dry well and a full well, and is a middle-aged play. I'm interested in doing a lecture at some stage on the empty and full, you know, the absence and presence. I think the interest in looking at fullness from an empty perspective, of wetness from a dry perspective, is a condition of changes in my life as much as anything else.

Perhaps the most interesting aspect of the tree's appearance in the poem is that its most vivid description is of a scene Heaney never witnessed, its demise. He imagines the "white chips" flying and the "sigh / And collapse of what luxuriated" so convincingly that one is tempted to believe in its literal truth. Indeed, this may be the great power of poetry, the ability to see in ways we cannot ordinarily see, to find truth in fiction. And so he also imagines its nonbeing: "Its heft and hush become a bright nowhere, / A soul ramifying and forever / Silent, beyond silence listened for." In this last sonnet, while never mentioning his mother (her absence from the poem becomes in its own right an emblem of the thing being described), the poet finds in the ruined tree a suitable image for his relationship to her memory, to the void her death opens up in his life. As the conclusion to the sequence, it provides a stunning example of the poetic heights to which Seamus Heaney has so often ascended in an already long and, from all evidence, still growing career.

Notes and References

Chapter One

1. Neil Corcoran, *Seamus Heaney* (London: Faber & Faber, 1986), 12.

2. *North* (New York: Oxford Univ. Press, 1975), 10; hereafter cited in the text as *N,* followed by page number(s).

3. Corcoran, *Seamus Heaney,* 19.

4. Ibid., 20–21.

5. *Preoccupations* (New York: Farrar, Straus & Giroux, 1980), 29; hereafter cited in the text as *P,* followed by page number(s).

6. Corcoran, *Seamus Heaney,* 22.

7. Ibid., 24.

8. Ibid., 37–38.

9. Ibid., 40.

10. Ibid., 41.

11. *Place and Displacement: Recent Poetry of Northern Ireland* (Grasmere: Trustees of Dove Cottage, 1985), 1; hereafter cited in the text as *P&D,* followed by page number(s).

Chapter Two

1. *Death of a Naturalist* (London: Faber & Faber, 1966), 29; hereafter cited in the text as *DN,* followed by page number(s).

2. *Station Island* (New York: Farrar, Straus & Giroux, 1984), 87; hereafter cited in the text as *SI,* followed by page number(s).

3. Corcoran, *Seamus Heaney,* 53.

4. Roland Mathias, "*Death of a Naturalist,*" in *The Art of Seamus Heaney,* ed. Tony Curtis (Chester Springs, Pa.: Dufour, 1985), 14.

5. Corcoran, *Seamus Heaney,* 45.

6. *Door into the Dark* (London: Faber & Faber, 1969), 19; hereafter cited in the text as *DD,* followed by page number(s).

7. Corcoran, *Seamus Heaney,* 56.

8. Robert Buttel, *Seamus Heaney* (Lewisburg, Pa.: Bucknell University Press, 1975), 49.

9. Christopher Ricks, *The Force of Poetry* (New York: Oxford University Press, 1984), 51–56.

10. Philip Hobsbaum, "Craft and Technique in *Wintering Out,*" in *The Art of Seamus Heaney,* 40.

Chapter Three

1. Heaney, *Wintering Out* (London: Faber & Faber, 1972), 48; hereafter cited in text as *WO,* followed by page number(s).

2. Blake Morrison, *Seamus Heaney* (London: Methuen, 1982), 42.

3. Hobsbaum, "Craft and Technique," 37–43.

4. *An Open Letter* (Derry: Field Day, 1983), 13.

5. Anne Stevenson, "*Stations:* Seamus Heaney and the Sacred Sense of the Sensitive Self," in *The Art of Seamus Heaney,* 48–51.

6. Corcoran, *Seamus Heaney,* 93.

7. *Stations* (Belfast: Honest Ulsterman, 1975), 9; hereafter cited in the text as *S,* followed by page number(s).

Chapter Four

1. Ciaran Carson, "Escaped from the Massacre?" *The Honest Ulsterman,* 50 (Winter 1975): 184–85.

2. Morrison, 68.

3. Corcoran, 115.

4. Ibid.

5. Ibid., 108.

6. Ibid., 109.

7. *Field Work* (London/Boston: Faber & Faber, 1979), 22; hereafter cited in the text as *FW,* followed by page number(s).

8. Corcoran, *Seamus Heaney,* 34.

9. Seamus Deane, "Unhappy and at Home: An Interview with Seamus Heaney," *The Crane Bag* 1, no. 1 (1977):52.

10. Ibid., 63.

11. John Haffenden, *Viewpoints: Poets in Conversation with John Haffenden* (London: Faber & Faber, 1981), 69–70.

12. Edna Longley, "*North:* 'Inner Emigré' or 'Artful Voyeur'?" in *The Art of Seamus Heaney,* 71.

Chapter Five

1. Corcoran, *Seamus Heaney,* 129.

2. Ibid., 145.

3. Ibid., 147.

Chapter Six

1. J. G. O'Keeffe, ed., *Buile Suibhne Geilt* (Dublin: Dublin Institute for Advanced Studies, 1931), xxx–xxxii.

2. Ibid., xxxiv.

3. *Sweeney Astray* (New York: Farrar, Straus & Giroux, 1984), vi; hereafter cited in the text as *SA,* followed by page number(s).

4. Ciaran Carson, "*Sweeney Astray:* Escaping from Limbo," in *The Art of Seamus Heaney,* 146–47.

5. Ibid., 147.

6. O'Keeffe, *Buile Suibhne Geilt,* 65.

7. Corcoran, *Seamus Heaney,* 179–80.

Chapter Seven

1. Barbary Hardy, "Meeting the Myth: *Station Island,*" in *The Art of Seamus Heaney,* 158.

2. Ibid., 153.

3. Morrison, *Seamus Heaney,* 19.

4. Robert B. Shaw, "Heaney's Purgatory," *Yale Review* 74 (July 1985): 581–87.

5. Nicholas Christopher, "A Pilgrim in County Donegal," *New York Times Book Review,* 10 March 1985, 9.

6. Helen Vendler, "Echo Soundings, Searches Probes," *New Yorker,* 23 September 1985, 108.

Chapter Eight

1. Heaney, *The Haw Lantern* (New York: Farrar, Straus & Giroux, 1987), 1; hereafter cited in the text as *HL,* followed by page number(s).

2. Neil Corcoran, "From the Frontier of Writing," *Times Literary Supplement,* 26 June 1987, 681.

Selected Bibliography

PRIMARY WORKS

Poetry

Death of a Naturalist. London: Faber & Faber, 1966.

Door into the Dark. London: Faber & Faber, 1969.

Eleven Poems. Belfast: Festival Publications, Queen's University, 1965.

Field Work. London / Boston: Faber & Faber, 1979.

Gravities: A Collection of Poems and Drawings. Newcastle-upon-Tyne: Charlotte Press, 1979.

Hailstones. Dublin: Gallery Books, 1984.

The Haw Lantern. London: Faber & Faber, 1987; New York: Farrar, Straus & Giroux, 1987.

North. London: Faber & Faber, 1975; New York: Oxford University Press, 1976.

An Open Letter. Derry: Field Day, 1983.

Poems 1965–75. New York: Farrar, Straus & Giroux, 1980.

Station Island. London: Faber & Faber, 1984; New York: Farrar, Straus & Giroux, 1985.

Stations. Belfast: Ulsterman Publications, 1975.

Sweeney Astray. Derry: Field Day, 1983; New York: Farrar, Straus & Giroux, 1984.

Essays and Lectures

"Envies and Identifications: Dante and the Modern Poet." *Irish University Review* 15, no. 1 (1985): 5–19.

The Fire i' the Flint: Reflections on the Poetry of Gerard Manley Hopkins. London: Oxford University Press, 1975.

Place and Displacement: Recent Poetry of Northern Ireland. Grasmere: Trustees of Dove Cottage, 1985

"The Placeless Heaven: Another Look at Kavanagh." *Massachusetts Review* 28, no. 3 (Autumn 1987): 371–80.

Preoccupations: Selected Prose 1968–78. London: Faber & Faber, 1980; New York: Farrar, Straus & Giroux, 1980.

The Rattle Bag. Co-edited with Ted Hughes. London: Faber & Faber, 1982.

Interviews

Deane, Seamus. "Talk with Seamus Heaney." *New York Times Book Review,* 2 December 1979, 79–101.

———. "Unhappy and at Home: An Interview with Seamus Heaney," *Crane Bag* 1, no. 1 (1977): 66–67.

Druce, Robert. "A Raindrop on a Thorn: An Interview with Seamus Heaney." *Dutch Quarterly Review* 9, no. 1 (1979): 24–37.

Haffenden, John, "Meeting Seamus Heaney: An Interview." In *Viewpoints: Poets in Conversation with John Haffenden,* 57–75. London: Faber & Faber, 1981.

Kinahan, Frank. "Artists on Art: An Interview with Seamus Heaney." *Critical Inquiry* 8, no. 3 (Spring 1983): 405–14.

Mooney, Bel. "Poet, pilgrim, fugitive . . . ." The Times Profile: Seamus Heaney, [London] *Times,* 11 October 1984, 8.

Randall, James. "An Interview with Seamus Heaney." *Ploughshares* 5, no. 3 (1979): 7–22.

SECONDARY WORKS

Checklists

Durkan, Michael J. "Seamus Heaney: A Checklist for a Bibliography." *Irish University Review* 16, no. 1 (Spring 1986): 48–76. The most comprehensive list of sources by and about Heaney, through late 1985.

Books and Parts of Books

Annwn, David. *Inhabited Voices: Myth and History in the Poetry of Geoffrey Hill, Seamus Heaney and George Mackay Brown.* Frome, Somerset: Bran's Head Books, 1984. Insightful readings of poems, particularly in *North,* studying the use of myth and history to inform the political awareness of the poems.

Brandley, Anthony. "Landscape as Culture: The Poetry of Seamus Heaney." In *Contemporary Irish Writing,* edited by J. D. Brophy and R. J. Porter, 1–14. Boston: Twayne Publishers, 1983. Studies the various uses of farms and bogs in the poetry through *Field Work.*

Broadbridge, Edward, ed. *Seamus Heaney.* Copenhagen: Radio Danmarks, 1977. Interesting, with text, interview, and photographs, but scant new material.

Brown, Terence. "Four New Voices: Poets of the Present." In *Northern Voices: Poets from Ulster.* Dublin: Gill and Macmillan, 1975, 171–213. Appreciative discussion of the early works.

Buttel, Robert. *Seamus Heaney.* Lewisburg: Bucknell University Press, 1975. Sensitive, although limited introduction to the first three books.

Corcoran, Neil. *Seamus Heaney.* London: Faber & Faber, 1986. The most comprehensive and most important study to date. Some excellent readings, along with a wealth of biographical and critical material.

Curtis, Tony, ed. *The Art of Seamus Heaney.* Bridgend: Poetry Wales Press, 1982. A variety of viewpoints, ranging from the openly admiring (Curtis) to the skeptical (Ciaran Carson) and covering all of Heaney's work up through *Station Island.*

King, P. R. *Nine Contemporary Poets.* London: Methuen, 1979. Appreciative introduction to the early work, through *North.*

McGuinness, Arthur E. "The Craft of Diction: Revision in Seamus Heaney's Poems." In *Image and Illusion: Anglo-Irish Literature and its Contexts,* edited by Maurice Harmon, 62–91. Portmarnock, Ireland: Wolfhound Press, 1979. As the title intimates, an analysis of the changes Heaney brings about in his poems from draft to draft.

Macrae, Alasdair. "Seamus Heaney's New Voice in *Station Island.*" In *Irish Writers and Society at Large,* edited by Masaru Sekine, 122–38. Gerrards Cross: Colin Smythe 1985; Totowa, N.J.: Barnes & Noble, 1985. Praises a wider range in the material as well as a dramatic mode in the presentation.

Morrison, Blake. *Seamus Heaney.* London: Methuen, 1982. Analysis of the poetry through *Field Work.* Useful sensible readings, although much of the information has been superceded by Corcoran.

Ricks, Christopher. *The Force of Poetry.* New York: Oxford University Press, 1984. See especially pages 51–56. A provocative comparison of certain rhetorical figures in Marvell and in contemporary Ulster poets, including Heaney.

Warner, Alan. "Seamus Heaney." *Guide to Anglo-Irish Literature, 260–68. Dublin: Gill and Macmillan, 1981, Informative encyclopedic entry.*

Watson, George. "The Narrow Ground: Northern Poets and the Northern Ireland Crisis." In *Irish Writers and Society at Large,* edited by Masaru Sekine, 207–24. Gerrards Cross: Colin Smythe 1985; Totowa, N.J.: Barnes & Noble, 1985. Places Heaney in the context of the Northern Troubles and within the group that includes Paulin, Mahon, and Longley.

Articles

Andrews, Elmer. "The Gift and the Craft: An Approach to the Poetry of Seamus Heaney." *Twentieth Century Literature* 31 (Winter 1985): 368–79. A study of the poetics, particularly of the middle work.

Clines, Francis X. "Poet of the Bogs: Seamus Heaney, Ireland's Foremost Living Poet Commands a Growing Audience." *New York Times Magazine,*

13 March 1983, 42–43, 98–99, 104. Profile piece aimed at general audience.

Corcoran, Neil. "From Frontier of Writing." *Times Literary Supplement,* 26 June 1987, 681–82. Review of *The Haw Lantern.*

Foster, John Wilson. "The Poetry of Seamus Heaney." *Critical Quarterly* 16 (Spring 1974): 35–48. An early discussion of the poems through *Wintering Out.*

Hildebidle, John, "A Decade of Seamus Heaney's Poetry." *Massachusetts Review* 28, no. 3 (Autumn 1987): 393–409. Another introduction, focusing on work from *North* to *Station Island.*

Lloyd, David. "Pap for the Dispossessed: Seamus Heaney and the Poetics of Identity." *Boundary 2* 13, nos. 2–3 (1985): 319–42. Discussion of his work as a Catholic minority poet.

Mahony, Philip. "Seamus Heaney and the Violence in Northern Ireland." *Journal of Irish Literature* 11, no. 3 (September 1982): 20–30. Traces responses to the Troubles in the poems, focusing especially on work of 1973–80.

Mason, David. "Seamus Heaney's Gutteral Muse." *Mid-American Review* 4, no. 2 (Fall 1984): 101–5. Brief discussion of Heaney's poetic language.

McClatchy, J. D. "The Exile's Song." *New Republic,* 21 December 1987, 36–39. Review of *The Haw Lantern.*

Meares, Peter. "Ah Poet, Lucky Poet: Seamus Heaney's *Station Island.*" *Agenda* 22 (Autumn–Winter 1984–85): 90–96. Review.

Murphy, Richard. "Poetry and Terror." *New York Review of Books,* 30 September 1976, 38–40. Review of *North.*

Niel, Ruth. "Digging into History: A Reading of Brian Friel's *Volunteers* and Seamus Heaney's 'Viking Dublin: Trial Pieces.' " *Irish University Review* 16, no. 1 (Spring 1986): 35–47. Interesting comparison of two emerging major figures' use of history on their work.

Parini, Jay. "Seamus Heaney: The Ground Possessed." *Southern Review* 16 (Winter 1980): 100–23. Analysis concentrating on interplay of history, oppression, and poetics, particularly in *North.*

Shaw, Robert B. "Heaney's Purgatory." *Yale Review* 74 (July 1985). 581–87. Review of *Station Island.*

Stallworthy, Jon. "The Poet as Archaeologist: W. B. Yeats and Seamus Heaney." *Review of English Studies* 33 (1982): 158–74. Contrasts uses of the past in two major poets.

Vendler, Helen. "The Music of What Happens." *New Yorker,* 28 September 1981, 146–57. Review of *Field Work, Preoccupations,* and *Poems 1965–75.*

———. "Echo Soundings, Searches, Probes." *New Yorker,* 23 September 1985, 108–16. Review of *Station Island.*

Waterman, Andrew. "Somewhere Out There, Beyond: The Poetry of Seamus Heaney and Derek Mahon." *PN Review* 8, no. 1 (1981): 39–47. Overview of poetry through *Field Work.*

Index